Literature in English

for Cambridge IGCSE™ and O Level

WORKBOOK

Russell Carey & Trish Miller

Third edition with Digital access

Shaftesbury Road, Cambridge CB2 8EA, United Kingdom

One Liberty Plaza, 20th Floor, New York, NY 10006, USA

477 Williamstown Road, Port Melbourne, VIC 3207, Australia

314–321, 3rd Floor, Plot 3, Splendor Forum, Jasola District Centre, New Delhi – 110025, India

103 Penang Road, #05–06/07, Visioncrest Commercial, Singapore 238467

Cambridge University Press & Assessment is a department of the University of Cambridge.

We share the University's mission to contribute to society through the pursuit of education, learning and research at the highest international levels of excellence.

www.cambridge.org
Information on this title: www.cambridge.org/9781009522687

© Cambridge University Press & Assessment 2026

This publication is in copyright. Subject to statutory exception and to the provisions of relevant collective licensing agreements, no reproduction of any part may take place without the written permission of Cambridge University Press & Assessment.

First published 2015
Second edition 2018
Third edition 2026
20 19 18 17 16 15 14 13 12 11 10 9 8 7 6 5 4 3 2 1

Printed in the Netherlands by Wilco BV

A catalogue record for this publication is available from the British Library

ISBN   978-1-109-52268-7   Workbook with Digital Access

Additional resources for this publication at www.cambridge.org/9781009522687

Cambridge University Press & Assessment has no responsibility for the persistence or accuracy of URLs for external or third-party internet websites referred to in this publication and does not guarantee that any content on such websites is, or will remain, accurate or appropriate.

For EU product safety concerns, contact us at Calle de José Abascal, 56, 1°, 28003 Madrid, Spain, or email eugpsr@cambridge.org.

Third-party websites and resources referred to in this publication are not endorsed.

Cambridge International Education material in this publication is reproduced under licence and remains the intellectual property of Cambridge University Press & Assessment.

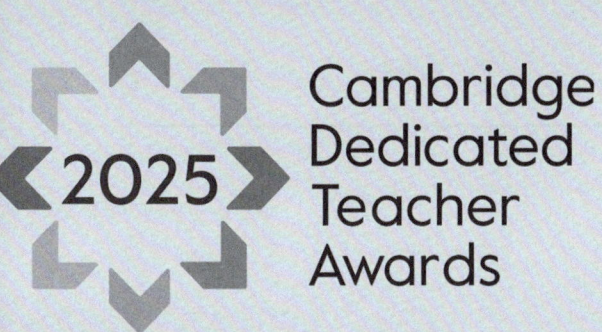

2025 Cambridge Dedicated Teacher Awards

Our **Cambridge Dedicated Teacher Awards** are an opportunity to show appreciation for the incredible work teachers do every day.

Thank you to everyone who nominated this year; we have been inspired and moved by all of your stories. Well done to all of our nominees for your dedication to learning and for inspiring the next generation of thinkers, leaders and innovators.

Congratulations to our winners!

Global Winner
Sub-Saharan Africa
Portia Dzilah
Pakro-Adjinase St. James Anglican Basic School, Ghana

East Asia
Yun Xie
Yew Wah International Education School of Shanghai Lingang, China

Europe
Oleksandr Zhuk
Zaporizhzhia Special Comprehensive Boarding Xchool, Dzherelo, Ukraine

Latin America
Eduardo Pérez
Instituto Técnico Guaimaral, Colombia

North America
Isabel de Feria
Marjory Stoneman Douglas Elementary, USA

Middle East and North Africa
Farrukh Saleem
Pakistan International School Jeddah English Section, Saudi Arabia

Pakistan
Adnan Ahmed Usmani
Bahria Town School and College, Pakistan

South Asia
Sakina Bharmal
The Galaxy School - Wadi, India

Southeast Asia & Pacific
Polly Neville
Denla British School Bangkok, Thailand

For more information about our dedicated teachers and their stories, go to **dedicatedteacher.cambridge.org**

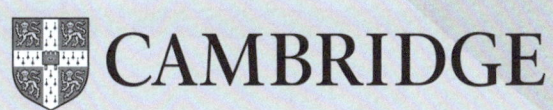

Endorsement statement

Endorsement indicates that a resource has passed Cambridge International Education's rigorous quality-assurance process and is suitable to support the delivery of their syllabus. However, endorsed resources are not the only suitable materials available to support teaching and learning, and are not essential to achieve the qualification. For the full list of endorsed resources to support this syllabus, visit www.cambridgeinternational.org/endorsed-resources

Any example answers to questions taken from past question papers, practice questions, accompanying marks and mark schemes included in this resource have been written by the authors and are for guidance only. They do not replicate examination papers. In examinations the way marks are awarded may be different. Any references to assessment and/or assessment preparation are the publisher's interpretation of the syllabus requirements. Examiners will not use endorsed resources as a source of material for any assessment set by Cambridge International Education.

While the publishers have made every attempt to ensure that advice on the qualification and its assessment is accurate, the official syllabus, specimen assessment materials and any associated assessment guidance materials produced by the awarding body are the only authoritative source of information and should always be referred to for definitive guidance.

Our approach is to provide teachers with access to a wide range of high-quality resources that suit different styles and types of teaching and learning.

For more information about the endorsement process, please visit www.cambridgeinternational.org/endorsed-resources

Cambridge International Education material in this publication is reproduced under licence and remains the intellectual property of Cambridge University Press & Assessment.

Third-party websites and resources referred to in this publication are not endorsed.

Contents

How to use this series	vi
How to use this book	vii

1 Approaching your course
- 1.1 Introduction — 1
- 1.2 Support for your study — 1

2 Responding to poetry
- 2.1 Reading poems closely and exploring meanings — 5
- 2.2 Exploring imagery and sound — 11
- 2.3 Looking closely at the effects created by writers — 15
- 2.4 Organising ideas in a sonnet — 19
- 2.5 Exploring free verse — 23
- 2.6 Exploring tone and mood — 28
- 2.7 Exploring voice — 34
- 2.8 Developing an informed personal response to a poem — 37

3 Responding to prose
- 3.1 Introducing prose — 42
- 3.2 Responding to how writers present characters — 44
- 3.3 Responding to theme — 50
- 3.4 Exploring setting and mood — 54
- 3.5 Exploring a first-person narrative — 58
- 3.6 Exploring a third-person narrative — 63
- 3.7 Developing an informed personal response to a short story — 66

4 Responding to drama
- 4.1 Exploring the ways in which dramatists portray characters — 70
- 4.2 Exploring language and effects — 75
- 4.3 Recapping a character from a drama text — 82
- 4.4 Writing a critical essay on your chosen character — 84
- 4.5 Exploring language and structure — 87
- 4.6 Exploring themes in a drama text — 91

5 Writing skills
- 5.1 Critical writing — 93
- 5.2 Approaching assessment — 97

Glossary	102
Acknowledgements	103

CAMBRIDGE IGCSE™ AND O LEVEL LITERATURE IN ENGLISH: WORKBOOK

> How to use this series

This suite of resources supports students and teachers following the Cambridge IGCSE™, IGCSE (9–1) and O Level Literature in English syllabuses (0475 / 0992 / 2010). All the components in the series are designed to work together and help students develop the necessary knowledge and skills for this subject.

This Coursebook is designed for students to use in class with guidance from the teacher or to be read as part of individual study. It is divided into six parts, which focus on the three genres of poetry, prose and drama, as well as writing skills and approaching assessment. Its purpose is to help students develop the skills necessary for a course in literature through a range of engaging activities and interesting text extracts. Reflection and Self-assessment features encourage students to think about their own learning, while Practice questions help to consolidate learning.

A digital version of the Coursebook is included with the print version and is available separately.

The write-in Workbook is skills-focused and consolidates the learning in the Coursebook providing opportunities for more focused practice. It follows a scaffolded approach to skills development, and can be used flexibly, as an additional resource to support learning in the classroom or at home for individual work. The Workbook fully reflects the structure of the Coursebook, making it easy to navigate.

A digital version of the Workbook is included with the print version.

The Digital Teacher's Resource is packed full of useful teaching notes and lesson ideas, with suggestions for differentiation to support and challenge students, ideas for assessment and homework. It offers guidance for all topics of the syllabus to help teachers plan and deliver the Coursebook units in the most effective, active way. Additional worksheets and text extract sheets are also available, to help teachers save time and enrich their practice. All answers to the Coursebook and Workbook activities are available on Cambridge GO.

> How to use this book

Throughout this book, you will notice different features that will help your learning. These are explained below.

Activities

These help you to practise skills that are important for studying Cambridge IGCSE and O Level Literature in English. They encourage you to reflect not only on the content of what you are reading, but also on the important role of the writer. Exploring the deliberate choices writers make in their writing will help you to improve your skills of analysis and increase your enjoyment of the texts you study.

1. Look out for activities with the set-text icon next to them. These are activities that you can apply to any of your set texts, to practise answering questions on.

> **SET TEXT ACTIVITY**
>
> These are skills-based activities that you can use independently alongside your set texts.

KEY TERMS

Key vocabulary is highlighted in the text when it is first introduced. An accompanying definition tells you the meanings of these words and phrases. You will also find definitions of these words in the Glossary at the end of the book.

Practice questions: Throughout each unit you'll find examples of practice questions written by the authors, alongside the number of marks available for a full answer. You'll practise your skills in planning answers and developing a personal response, which will provide preparation for responding to the type of task required by the syllabus.

> **SAMPLE ANSWER**
>
> Sample answers at a range of levels provide you with the opportunity to assess and reflect on what makes a successful answer. You can use these to help you to evaluate your own work and understand the success criteria. These sample answers have been written by the authors.

> Unit 1

Approaching your course

1.1 Introduction

This Workbook will help you develop the skills you need to succeed in Cambridge IGCSE™ or O Level Literature in English. It has been written for use alongside the Cambridge IGCSE and O Level Literature in English Coursebook third edition.

In this Workbook you will find a rich variety of texts from a wide range of writers. These include poems and extracts from drama and prose fiction texts. Some of the texts in this Workbook can also be found in the Coursebook, though the activities are different. Many of the texts are completely new and are ones that you may not have come across before.

The activities in this Workbook ask the sorts of questions you need to ask as you analyse literary texts. There is an initial section of study support with guidance on active learning, essay writing and further reading; then the rest of the Workbook is divided into three main sections:

- Responding to poetry
- Responding to prose
- Responding to drama.

These sections are followed by a final section on consolidating your writing skills and approaching assessment, which complements the corresponding Parts in the Coursebook, and which give you a final opportunity to study a poem and a prose extract.

All these sections will help you develop and practise the skills you need for understanding and exploring texts – and communicating your responses effectively. Remember that in studying English literature, you will make progress over time. If you work conscientiously through the activities in this Workbook as well as those in the Coursebook, they will help you to acquire the skills you need for success in this subject.

1.2 Support for your study

Active learning

If you are to get the most out of your Literature in English course, you need to build your confidence in expressing your personal response to the poems, plays and prose fiction you read.

There is no such thing as a 'correct' or 'model' answer in this subject. It is not your teacher's role to provide you with prepared approaches to answering questions that might be set on the ideas, characters or settings you will encounter in the texts you study. This would not, in fact, be helpful for you nor would it improve your own ability to respond to literature.

It is therefore important that you are an active learner. The checklist in Table 1.1 should help you find out just how much of an active learner you are. Tick the column that applies to you.

Do I . . .	Always	Sometimes	Never
prepare for lessons by reading ahead from set texts?			
re-read and review after lessons what I have studied in class?			
consult a dictionary to look up unfamiliar words?			
make notes in lessons and as I read?			
annotate copies of poems or pages from longer prose or drama texts?			
research set texts online?			
practise reading aloud poems and extracts from longer texts?			
consider other students' views in order to confirm or challenge my own?			

Table 1.1: Active learner checklist

If you have more ticks in the 'Always' column, well done! If any ticks appear in the 'Sometimes' or 'Never' columns, you should reflect on what you need to do to become a fully active learner.

> **KEY TERM**
>
> **annotate:** to make notes, providing brief explanations or comments

Wider reading

The more you read, the more you will find reading enjoyable. Over time, you will discover hundreds of new words. These will be available to you for the rest of your life and in a very real sense become a part of who you are. You will also become familiar with the different styles of writers and be able to enjoy a range of exciting and interesting texts.

The Coursebook includes lists of texts that are often read by students of your age. Look out for the 'Further reading' boxes in the Coursebook for good suggestions. Teachers and others may also recommend books for you to read. You can find other ideas online, in newspapers and magazines, and on radio and television.

Checklist for writing critical essays

Use the checklist in Table 1.2, and the mind map in Figure 1.1, to check whether you have considered all the important key points for writing an effective essay.

This checklist, and the mind map, can be used to help you plan and write any formal essays during your Literature in English course. If you use them regularly, you should become increasingly confident about writing essays.

Tick	Have I...	Guidance
	made sure that all my points are focused on the actual question?	Don't write for a question you wanted to be set and may have prepared for. Make sure you answer the actual question. Leave out material that is not relevant to the question, even if it shows how detailed your general understanding of the text is.
	used paragraphs and connectives to make my argument clear to the reader?	Paragraphs and connectives (words such as 'however', 'therefore' and 'in addition') help you to structure your essays effectively and ensure your points flow in a logical sequence.
	used accurate spelling and punctuation?	Accurate use of English enables the reader to concentrate on the content of your essay without being distracted by errors.
	written in formal English?	Avoid informal English such as contractions (for example, 'don't', 'can't', 'isn't'). Avoid slang or clichés (for example, 'He was gutted when he lost'; 'She thought the grass was always greener on the other side').
	used quotations and references to the text to support my points?	You need to support your points and ideas by using evidence from the text. If you don't do this, your views are merely assertions (statements that you may think are true but which you have not provided any evidence for).
	integrated quotations smoothly into my writing?	Quotations should be brief and contain only the word or phrase you wish to comment on as part of your analysis. Short quotations are easier to insert smoothly into the flow of your own writing. Remember always to use quotation marks.
	analysed **structure**?	In poetry questions and extract-based drama questions you can explore the structure of the printed poem or extract. In general essays you might explore aspects of characters, themes or settings at different stages of the text. In poems this can include the length of lines or how the poem begins and ends.
	analysed the language?	It is important to comment on the effects for a reader (or audience of a play) of any words or phrases that you quote. This is a key part of literary analysis.
	commented on **form**?	It needs to be clear from your essays that you are responding to texts written in particular literary forms: poems, plays or prose fiction.

Table 1.2: Writing critical essays checklist

> **KEY TERMS**
>
> **structure:** how ideas are organised and arranged in a text to achieve effects
>
> **form:** the distinctive features of poetry, drama or prose fiction

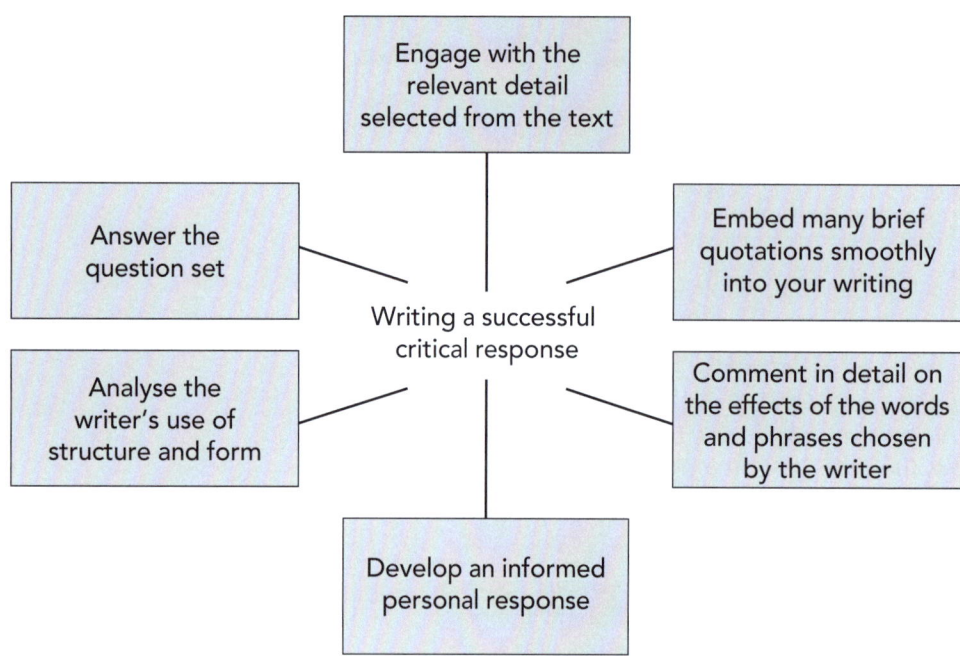

Figure 1.1: Writing a successful critical response

Unit 2
Responding to poetry

2.1 Reading poems closely and exploring meanings
'The Owl' by Edward Thomas

Edward Thomas wrote his poems between 1914 and 1917, when he was killed in the First World War. Although his poems are not always as explicitly about the experience of war, they are very much aware of the presence of war in the background and how it affects individuals.

The Owl

Downhill I came, hungry, and yet not starved;
Cold, yet had heat within me that was proof
Against the North wind; tired, yet so that rest
Had seemed the sweetest thing under a roof.

Then at the inn I had food, fire, and rest,   5
Knowing how hungry, cold, and tired was I.
All of the night was quite barred out except
An owl's cry, a most melancholy cry

Shaken out long and clear upon the hill,
No merry note, nor cause of merriment,   10
But one telling me plain what I escaped
And others could not, that night, as in I went.

And salted was my food, and my repose,
Salted and sobered, too, by the bird's voice
Speaking for all who lay under the stars,   15
Soldiers and poor, unable to rejoice.

CAMBRIDGE IGCSE™ AND O LEVEL LITERATURE IN ENGLISH: WORKBOOK

1 Read the poem carefully and look up any words you are not completely confident about. Underline the word and write the meaning next to it.

2 Look carefully at lines 1–6. How is the narrator feeling at this moment in the poem? What evidence can you find for this in these lines?

....

....

....

....

3 Now consider in detail how the speaker's attitude changes in lines 7–12.

   a What **metaphor** is used in line 7 to describe his thoughts before he hears the owl, and what does this mean?

   ....

   ....

   b What are the effects of the words used to describe the owl's cry in lines 8–10?

   ....

   ....

   ....

   ....

   ....

   c Lines 11–12 convey how the speaker's thoughts change. In your own words, explain their meaning.

   ....

   ....

   ....

   ....

> **KEY TERM**
>
> **metaphor:** a literary device that says that one thing is actually another, rather than using words such as 'like' to compare things. For example, in Wilfred Owen's poem 'Exposure', the burning coal in fires is described as 'dark-red jewels'

2 Responding to poetry

4 In the final **stanza**, the speaker makes it even clearer how he has been changed by hearing the owl.

> **KEY TERM**
>
> **stanza:** a group of lines within a poem

    a Explain what he is now thinking and feeling, using quotations from the poem.

....

....

....

....

    b Explore how this reveals the deeper meanings of the poem.

....

....

....

....

5 Look more closely at the language used.

    a Find **one** example where Thomas repeats words. What effect does he create?

....

....

....

....

    b Choose **one** word or short phrase from each stanza that you think is particularly important in conveying the deeper meanings of the poem. Explain what impact it has on the reader in Table 2.1.

Stanza	Word/phrase	Impact on the reader
1		
2		
3		
4		

Table 2.1: Impact of words/phrases on readers in 'The Owl'

6 Look at the following statements and pair them up under the correct heading in Table 2.2. There are five surface meanings and five corresponding deeper meanings. An example has been given for you.

- The speaker is quite hungry, tired and cold as he walks along.
- The owl is the 'voice' which speaks for those who cannot be heard.
- His needs are very easily and quickly met at the inn.
- He hears an owl's cry, which he finds quite sad.
- He is just uncomfortable, not really in a bad situation.
- He doesn't need or want any difficult thoughts to disturb him.
- The cold, dark night is shut out when he is in the inn.
- His food is in contrast to those who are suffering at war or in great need.
- He is given food, warmth and rest when he arrives at the inn.
- His food is nicely seasoned and tasty.

Surface meaning	Deeper meaning
The speaker is quite hungry, tired and cold as he walks along.	He is just uncomfortable, not really in a bad situation.

Table 2.2: Surface and deeper meanings in 'The Owl'

7 Look at this practice question:

> **How does Thomas strikingly convey the thoughts and feelings of the speaker in 'The Owl'? Support your ideas with details from the text.** [25]

Make notes based on your answers to activities 1–6 and then write a clear plan, focusing on how the speaker's thoughts and feelings change as he moves from outside into the inn and then hears the owl's cry. Remember to use **brief** quotations from the poem to support your points.

SET TEXT ACTIVITY 1

Choose **one** of the poems you are studying which you think has a powerful ending. Explain what makes the ending powerful. How does it help you to understand the deeper meanings of the poem?

2.2 Exploring imagery and sound

'The Lady of Shalott', Part II, by Alfred, Lord Tennyson

'I am half-sick of shadows' by John William Waterhouse

The Lady of Shalott

Part II

No time hath she to sport and play:
A charmed web she weaves alway[1].
A curse is on her, if she stay[2]
Her weaving, either night or day,
    To look down to Camelot.   5
She knows not what the curse may be;
Therefore she weaveth steadily,
Therefore no other care hath she,
    The Lady of Shalott.

She lives with little joy or fear.   10
Over the water, running near,
The sheepbell tinkles in her ear.
Before her hangs a mirror clear,
    Reflecting tower'd Camelot.
And as the mazy[3] web she whirls,   15
She sees the surly village churls[4],
And the red cloaks of market girls
    Pass onward from Shalott.

Sometimes a troop of damsels[5] glad,
An abbot[6] on an ambling pad,   20
Sometimes a curly shepherd lad,
Or long-hair'd page[7] in crimson clad,
    Goes by to tower'd Camelot:
And sometimes thro' the mirror blue
The knights come riding two and two: 25
She hath no loyal knight and true,
    The Lady of Shalott.

GLOSSARY

[1] **alway:** always

[2] **stay:** stops

[3] **mazy:** complex, intricate

[4] **churls:** rude young men

[5] **damsels:** young women

[6] **abbot:** priest

[7] **page:** a boy who serves a knight

CAMBRIDGE IGCSE™ AND O LEVEL LITERATURE IN ENGLISH: WORKBOOK

> But in her web she still delights
> To weave the mirror's magic sights,
> For often thro' the silent nights   30
> A funeral, with plumes and lights
>   And music, came from Camelot:
> Or when the moon was overhead
> Came two young lovers lately wed;
> 'I am half sick of shadows,' said   35
>   The Lady of Shalott.

You can find Part I of this poem in Unit 5 of the Coursebook. You should complete Activity 9 in the Coursebook before attempting activities 1–5 here.

1 Read Part I of the poem from the Coursebook to refresh your memory. Then read Part II here and look up any words you are unsure of. Write brief explanations for these words next to where they appear in the poem.

You will see that in Part II the plot moves on and much more of the meaning is made clear. Read Part II aloud to capture the rhythm of the poem again.

2 Summarise what you learn of the Lady of Shalott's situation in stanza 1. Use your own words as far as possible.

....

....

....

....

....

....

....

....

....

....

....

2 Responding to poetry

3 Stanzas 2 and 3 describe what the Lady of Shalott sees reflected in the mirror.

Look at the clues the poem gives you about her feelings in line 10 and line 26.
Explain what her feelings are and provide a supporting quotation in Table 2.3.

Line	The Lady's feelings	Supporting quotation
10		
26		

Table 2.3: Evidence of the Lady's feelings in 'The Lady of Shalott'

4 Look at lines 28–34 in stanza 4.

  a What do you learn about the Lady of Shalott's life?

  ....

  ....

  ....

  ....

  b How does the poet use **alliteration** in these lines to emphasise the use of sound imagery in the poem?

  ....

  ....

  ....

  ....

  c The Lady's weaving is called a 'web'. What effect does this metaphor create?

  ....

  ....

  ....

  ....

> **KEY TERM**
>
> **alliteration:** the repetition of consonant sounds in words that are close together. For example, '**S**udden **s**ucce**ss**ive fligh**ts** of bulle**ts** **s**treak the **s**ilence'

5   Look at the final two lines of Part II.

   a   How do these lines create a striking ending to this section of the poem?

   ....

   ....

   ....

   ....

   ....

   ....

   b   How does the word 'shadows' help you to understand what the Lady is feeling?

   ....

   ....

   ....

   ....

   ....

   ....

Refer now to the Coursebook, which suggests activities to complete your reading of Parts III and IV of the poem as a class.

2.3 Looking closely at the effects created by writers

'Home after Three Months Away' by Robert Lowell

Robert Lowell (1917–1977) was an American poet. Many of his poems focus on his personal struggles. He spent time with depression in psychiatric hospitals throughout his adult life and this undoubtedly influenced his poetry.

Home after Three Months Away

Gone now the baby's nurse,
a lioness who ruled the roost
and made the Mother cry.
She used to tie
gobbets[1] of porkrind in bowknots[2] of gauze — 5
three months they hung like soggy toast
on our eight foot magnolia tree,
and helped the English sparrows
weather a Boston winter.

Three months, three months! 10
Is Richard now himself again?
Dimpled with exaltation,
my daughter holds her levee[3] in the tub.
Our noses rub,
each of us pats a stringy lock of hair — 15
they tell me nothing's gone.
Though I am forty-one,
not forty now, the time I put away
was child's-play. After thirteen weeks
my child still dabs her cheeks 20
to start me shaving. When
we dress her in her sky-blue corduroy,
she changes to a boy,
and floats my shaving brush
and washcloth in the flush. . . . 25
Dearest, I cannot loiter here
in lather like a polar bear.

GLOSSARY

[1] **gobbets:** small pieces

[2] **bowknots:** decorative knots

[3] **levee:** bath-time

Recuperating, I neither spin nor toil.
Three stories[4] down below,
a choreman tends our coffin's length of soil, 30
and seven horizontal tulips blow.
Just twelve months ago,
these flowers were pedigreed
imported Dutchmen, now no one need
distinguish them from weed. 35
Bushed by the late spring snow,
they cannot meet
another year's snowballing enervation.[5]

I keep no rank nor station.
Cured, I am frizzled, stale and small. 40

GLOSSARY

[4] **stories:** floors of buildings (in US English) 'storeys' (floors)

[5] **enervation:** a feeling of being drained of energy

1   Find the following information from the poem:

    a How old is the speaker at the time of writing the poem?

    ....

    b How long has he been away from home?

    ....

2   Read lines 1–9. What impressions do you form of the baby's nurse? Use brief quotations to support your answer.

2 Responding to poetry

3 Look at stanzas 1 and 2 (lines 1–27).

   a What evidence is there that the speaker has been ill and away from home?

       ....

       ....

       ....

       ....

       ....

       ....

   b How does the poet use language to reveal his thoughts about being away from home?

       ....

       ....

       ....

       ....

       ....

       ....

       ....

4 What does the writing in stanza 2 (lines 10–27) vividly reveal about the relationship between father and daughter? Use brief quotations to support your answer.

   ....

   ....

   ....

   ....

   ....

   ....

   ....

5 What do you think is the significance of the tulips described in stanza 3 (lines 29–38)? Give reasons for your answer.

....

....

....

....

....

....

6 What do you find effective about the following phrases or lines? Use a dictionary if you need to.

    a   Dimpled with exaltation, (line 12)

....

....

....

    b   . . . the time I put away

           was child's-play. (lines 18–19)

....

....

....

    c   Dearest, I cannot loiter here

           in lather like a polar bear. (lines 26–27)

....

....

....

    d   Recuperating, I neither spin nor toil. (line 28)

....

....

....

7   Consider the impact of the poem's final two lines. What are your final impressions of the father?

> I keep no rank nor station.
>
> Cured, I am frizzled, stale and small. (lines 39–40)

....

....

....

....

....

2.4 Organising ideas in a sonnet
'Sonnet' by Elizabeth Bishop

Elizabeth Bishop (1911–1979) was an American poet. Interestingly, she had a close friendship with Robert Lowell, the previous poet you studied in the Workbook. They exchanged hundreds of letters, often discussing and influencing each other's work.

In this **sonnet**, the speaker writes about the magical qualities of music and what music means to her.

KEY TERM

sonnet: a poem of 14 lines, each having 10 syllables

Sonnet

I am in need of music that would flow
Over my fretful, feeling fingertips,
Over my bitter-tainted, trembling lips,
With melody, deep, clear, and liquid-slow.
Oh, for the healing swaying, old and low,   5
Of some song sung to rest the tired dead,
A song to fall like water on my head,
And over quivering limbs, dream flushed to glow!

There is a magic made by melody:
A spell of rest, and quiet breath, and cool   10
Heart, that sinks through fading colors deep
To the subaqueous[1] stillness of the sea,
And floats forever in a moon-green pool,
Held in the arms of rhythm and of sleep.

GLOSSARY

[1] **subaqueous:** underwater

1   Read the poem carefully. Then read Unit 5.3 of the Coursebook to remind yourself of the sonnet form.

    Look at the sonnet's **octave** (lines 1–8). Explain briefly why the speaker is 'in need of music'.

    To help you answer, you might consider lines 2–3.

    ....

    ....

    ....

    ....

> **KEY TERM**
>
> **octave:** the first eight lines of a sonnet

2   In the octave, the speaker makes the contrast clear between her current mood and the music she desires.

    Complete Figure 2.1, a mind map, adding quotations to show what the differences are. Two quotations have been added to get you started.

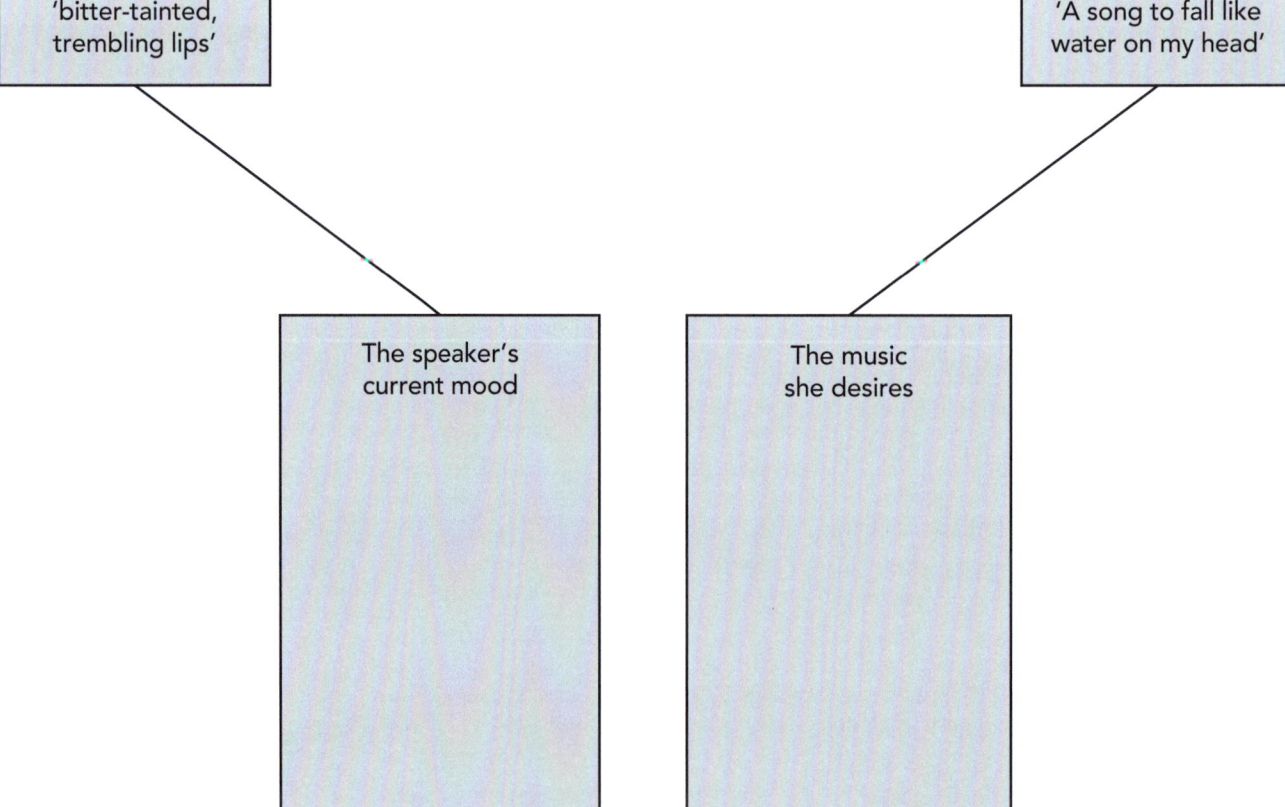

Figure 2.1: Contrasts in the speaker's current mood and the music she desires in 'I Am In Need Of Music'

2 Responding to poetry

 3 Find **one** example of **imagery** and one sound device used in lines 1–8, and write your answer in Table 2.4. Then comment on the effects Bishop creates in her presentation of the speaker.

	Example	Effect
Imagery		
Sound device		

Table 2.4: Devices and their effects in 'I Am In Need Of Music'

4 As you read the **sestet** (lines 9–14), you will notice a shift in the content and mood of the poem. In your own words, explain what the speaker means by 'There is a magic made by melody' (in line 9).

....

....

5 Explore how the speaker uses words, images and sounds in lines 9–14 to convey her love of music and its impact on her.

Highlight on the poem itself the key words in this section of the poem. Then complete your answer below, using short quotations to support your analysis.

....

....

....

....

....

> **KEY TERMS**
>
> **imagery:** a literary device where writers use vivid description to appeal to the reader's senses and create images in their mind. It plays a central role in poetry
>
> **sestet:** the final six lines of a sonnet

....

....

....

....

....

6 The rhyming of the words 'cool' and 'pool' help to support the idea of the 'melody' referred to in line 9. Comment on the effect created by one other pair of rhyming words.

The rhyming words:

....

Explanation:

....

....

....

....

2.5 Exploring free verse
'300 Goats' by Naomi Shihab Nye

Naomi Shihab Nye is an American poet and novelist, born in 1952 to a Palestinian father and American mother. She began writing poetry at the age of six.

This poem is written in **free verse**, having no regular lines or rhyme. It particularly suits the conversational tone of the poem and more natural rhythms of the voice.

> **KEY TERM**
>
> **free verse:** poetry with no regular rhyming pattern, line length or rhythm. This is the most common form in more modern poetry

300 Goats

In icy fields.
Is water flowing in the tank?
Will they huddle together, warm bodies pressing?
(Is it the year of the goat or the sheep?
Scholars debating Chinese zodiac[1], 5
follower or leader.)
O lead them to a warm corner,
little ones toward bulkier bodies.
Lead them to the brush, which cuts the icy wind.
Another frigid night swooping down — 10
Aren't you worried about them? I ask my friend,
who lives by herself on the ranch of goats,
far from here near the town of Ozona[2].
She shrugs, 'Not really,
they know what to do. They're *goats*.' 15

GLOSSARY

[1] **Chinese zodiac:** a 12-year repeating cycle based on the Chinese calendar, where each year is given the name of an animal

[2] **Ozona:** a town in Texas, USA

1   The short first line of the poem immediately describes the setting.
    Draw a circle around any of the following words that capture the tone.
    You can choose more than one:

    freezing   pretty   threatening   refreshing   bleak   safe   gloomy

2   The word 'icy' is used twice in the poem. Find another word in the poem which describes the severe cold.

    ....

3   In lines 2–3, the questions show that the speaker is worried about the goats' survival.

    a   What is the effect of these **rhetorical questions**?

        ....

        ....

    b   Find another question that shows her worry.

        ....

4   Lines 4–6 are in brackets and consider the 'Chinese zodiac'.
    Why do you think this is included in the poem? Line 6 gives a clue.

    ....

    ....

KEY TERM

rhetorical question: a type of question that does not require an answer, since this is usually obvious from the question. The purpose of a rhetorical question is to emphasise a point

5   a   Write the line which suggests that the speaker is praying for the safety of the goats.

    ....

    b   Write the line where the poet uses alliteration to emphasise the protection given by the bigger goats.

    ....

    c   Which line **personifies** the cold? What is the effect of this imagery?

    ....

    ....

> **KEY TERM**
>
> **personification:** when something inanimate is given human characteristics. For example, 'Our brains ache, in the merciless iced east winds that knive us'

6   Put a tick next to any of the following statements which you think expresses one of the poem's deeper meanings. Then choose (with a double tick) the two that you consider have the most impact on the reader. If you can, discuss your choice in a group or as a class.

We all need to stick together when times get tough.	
Goats are usually cleverer than sheep.	
Nature can have a sudden impact on our lives.	
It is important to have adequate shelter.	
It's foolish to be far away from home if you have animals there.	
Every group or community needs a strong leader.	
People have different views on how we should feel about animals.	
Try to take care of weaker people.	
Always be prepared for extremes of weather.	
Some people and communities are more resilient (strong, able to cope) than others.	

> CAMBRIDGE IGCSE™ AND O LEVEL LITERATURE IN ENGLISH: WORKBOOK

SET TEXT ACTIVITY 2

Choose a poem that has concern for other people, animals or the environment as a theme.

Write a paragraph about your chosen poem, making sure that you include quotations from the poem to support your ideas.

....

....

....

....

....

....

....

....

....

....

....

....

7 Free verse can sometimes read rather like prose simply split up into shorter lines!

    a   Rewrite this poem as a piece of prose, making sure that you convey the speaker's anxiety and the contrasting attitude of her friend.

The rules are:

- Write in the third person.
- Move words and ideas around – they don't have to be in the same order as the poem.
- Leave out words and ideas if they don't seem suitable or don't add anything to your writing.
- Add words and phrases if they seem necessary or make your ideas clearer.
- Only use **up to 100 words**, so make every word count!

For example, you could begin: 'A woman, who lives on a ranch in Texas, went to meet her friend.'

Afterwards, if you can, compare the differences of your writing with other students.

....

....

....

....

....

....

....

....

....

b The poem 'Orbit' in Unit 5.4 of the Coursebook provides another good example of free verse. Read the introduction to this poem, which explains more about why poets use free verse.

Table 2.5 lists comments made about 'Orbit'. Find examples from '300 Goats' that match these.

Comment	Example from '300 Goats'
Uses natural speech and thoughts	
Is able to convey strong emotions	
Isolates meaningful words or phrases for emphasis	

Table 2.5: Features of free verse in '300 Goats'

2.6 Exploring tone and mood

'Out, Out—' by Robert Frost

Robert Frost (1874–1963) became one of the most popular American poets of his time, winning four Pulitzer Prizes. Many of his poems are set in New England, in the East of the United States, and depict aspects of rural life, as in 'Out, Out—'.

> **'Out, Out—'**
>
> The buzz-saw snarled and rattled in the yard
> And made dust and dropped stove-length sticks of wood,
> Sweet-scented stuff when the breeze drew across it.
> And from there those that lifted eyes could count
> Five mountain ranges one behind the other   5
> Under the sunset far into Vermont.
> And the saw snarled and rattled, snarled and rattled,
> As it ran light, or had to bear a load.
> And nothing happened: day was all but done.
> Call it a day, I wish they might have said   10
> To please the boy by giving him the half hour
> That a boy counts so much when saved from work.
> His sister stood beside them in her apron
> To tell them 'Supper.' At the word, the saw,

As if to prove saws knew what supper meant, 15
Leaped out at the boy's hand, or seemed to leap-
He must have given the hand. However it was,
Neither refused the meeting. But the hand!
The boy's first outcry was a rueful laugh,
As he swung toward them holding up the hand 20
Half in appeal, but half as if to keep
The life from spilling. Then the boy saw all-
Since he was old enough to know, big boy
Doing a man's work, though a child at heart-
He saw all spoiled. 'Don't let him cut my hand off- 25
The doctor, when he comes. Don't let him, sister!'
So. But the hand was gone already.
The doctor put him in the dark of ether.
He lay and puffed his lips out with his breath.
And then-the watcher at his pulse took fright. 30
No one believed. They listened at his heart.
Little-less-nothing!-and that ended it.
No more to build on there. And they, since they
Were not the one dead, turned to their affairs.

1 Read the poem carefully so that you are familiar with the 'story' of the poem. Note how the mood changes at different points in the poem.

2 Frost deliberately leads the reader in clear stages towards the ending.

   a In lines 1–8, the speaker describes the pleasant smell of the wood, the beautiful scenery and the sunset, signalling the end of the working day.

   What word or words would you use to describe the tone and mood in this part of the poem?

   ....

   b How does line 10 create the first change in mood?

   ....

   c Lines 14–18 describe the terrible accident. Choose a word or words that now convey the mood of the poem.

   ....

d Lines 19–26 describe the boy's reaction. What are the changing tones of his voice in these lines?

....

e The doctor arrives to care for the boy in line 28. What moods are then created in the final five lines? Find three different moods and give brief quotations to support your ideas in Table 2.6.

Mood	Quotation

Table 2.6: Moods in 'Out, Out—'

f What do you think is the meaning and effect of the poem's title?

Meaning:

....

....

....

Effect:

....

....

....

3 Frost uses imagery to set the initial tone and to increase the impact of the boy's accident on the reader.

a In Table 2.7, write the following devices against the correct quotation then comment on their effects in the poem.

> **assonance** **onomatopoeia** personification alliteration

Quotation	Device	Effect
'The buzz-saw snarled and rattled' (line 1)		
'Sweet-scented stuff' (line 3)		
'Sweet . . . breeze' (line 3)		
'saws knew what supper meant' (line 15)		

Table 2.7: Devices and their effects in 'Out, Out—'

b Find **two** examples of repetition in the poem and explain their effect.

1 ....
....

2 ....
....

4 Frost uses **caesura** and **enjambment** effectively to give more impact to the mood and meaning of the poem.

a What is the effect of the single word and caesura 'So.' on line 27?

....
....

KEY TERMS

assonance: the repetition of vowel sounds in words which are placed close together

onomatopoeia: a word that sounds like the thing it describes. For example, 'buzz' in 'The bee buzzed in my ear'

caesura: a deliberate pause or stop in a line of poetry

enjambment: where lines run on without punctuation and without a break in the meaning

SAMPLE ANSWER

b The following are comments about the caesura and enjambment in the poem in lines 21–34. Put a tick against those which make a useful comment on the effect of these.

1. The caesura in lines 21–22 after 'to keep/ The life from spilling' is effective because it suggests that the boy's life might also have come to an end, like the sentence. ☐

2. The full stop after 'all spoiled' works well because it means both the reader and the boy stop and think about how his life has been so suddenly ruined by the accident. ☐

3. The caesura in line 25 is good because it makes a break in the story. ☐

4. When the poet writes 'Little-less-nothing!' he is using caesura to lead up to the moment when there is no pulse and so the boy has died at the same time as the sentence finishes. ☐

5. Lots of the sentences at the end of the poem end in full stops, which is really effective because it makes you stop and think, and you have to read it slowly. ☐

6. There is enjambment in lines 33–34 and this is so that you finish the poem quickly and the lines flow well to get the meaning across. ☐

7. The poet uses enjambment in the poem's final two lines to emphasise how the people who have been watching just 'turned to their affairs', as life has to go on for them. It is a contrast to the lines ending in caesura which go before, when there is still so much tension and everyone is holding their breath to see if he will live. ☐

5 The boy is described in four different ways in the poem. Put these in the order in which they occur in the poem and say what the effect of this is.

| man | big boy | child | boy |

....
....
....
....
....

6 In one way, this poem can be read as a straightforward but heart-rending story of everyday life on a farm in the early 20th century.

Two deeper meanings might be whether a boy (we don't know his exact age) should be given 'a man's work', and how much children should be 'saved from work'.

The final two lines suggest a third deeper meaning. If you can, discuss in pairs what these lines suggest.

Write a paragraph giving your personal response to one of these deeper meanings of the poem. You should give your own ideas about the poem's deeper meaning, but it is also important to support these from the text.

....
....
....
....
....
....
....
....

SET TEXT ACTIVITY 3

Choose one of your set text poems which has a change of tone or mood at some point. Identify exactly where this happens (it could be at more than one place) and write the different moods with the quotations that show this.

....
....
....
....
....

2.7 Exploring voice

'The Best of School' by D. H. Lawrence

> **GLOSSARY**
> [1] **blouses:** shirts
> [2] **laves:** washes

This poem can be compared with another D. H. Lawrence poem, 'Last Lesson of the Afternoon', in Unit 5.6 of the Coursebook. In that poem, the speaker expresses his frustration with the lesson and the students he teaches, creating a very bleak mood. The poem below conveys a completely different mood, as the title suggests. This poem has a strikingly different 'voice'.

The Best of School

The blinds are drawn because of the sun,
And the boys and the room in a colourless gloom
Of underwater float: bright ripples run
Across the walls as the blinds are blown
To let the sunlight in; and I,   5
As I sit on the shores of the class, alone,
Watch the boys in their summer blouses[1]
As they write, their round heads busily bowed:
And one after another rouses
His face to look at me;   10
To ponder very quietly,
As seeing, he does not see.

And then he turns again, with a little, glad
Thrill of his work he turns again from me,
Having found what he wanted, having got what was to be had.   15

And very sweet it is, while the sunlight waves
In the ripening morning, to sit alone with the class
And feel the stream of awakening ripple and pass
From me to the boys, whose brightening souls it laves[2]
For this little hour.   20

    This morning, sweet it is
To feel the lads' looks light on me,
Then back in a swift, bright flutter to work;
Each one darting away with his
Discovery, like birds that steal and flee.   25

Touch after touch I feel on me
As their eyes glance at me for the grain
Of rigour they taste delightedly.

2 Responding to poetry

> As tendrils³ reach out yearningly,
> Slowly rotate till they touch the tree   30
> That they cleave unto, and up which they climb
> Up to their lives—so they to me.
>
> I feel them cling and cleave to me
> As vines going eagerly up; they twine
> My life with other leaves, my time   35
> Is hidden in theirs, their thrills are mine.

GLOSSARY

³ **tendrils:** small thin stems

1. Read the poem carefully, and then summarise what is happening in it.

   ....

   ....

   ....

   ....

2. Twice the speaker describes himself as 'alone'. But the poem suggests the speaker (the teacher) has a powerful impact on the pupils just by being present in the classroom.

   Find and list in Table 2.8 **three** lines which show the teacher's influence on the pupils and their learning. An example has been provided for you.

Line(s) from the poem	What it shows about the teacher's influence
'And one after another rouses His face to look at me' (lines 9–10)	The students look to the teacher for inspiration

Table 2.8: The teacher's influence in 'The Best of School'

3 How effective do you find the extended metaphor of the 'tendrils' (lines 29–36)? Refer to other words and phrases in these lines to support your answer. Remember to make your quotations as concise as possible and use inverted commas around them.

....

....

....

....

....

....

....

....

....

....

4 Compare the ways in which the poet captures the voice of the teacher in this poem and in his other poem about school, 'Last Lesson of the Afternoon' (in Unit 5.6 of the Coursebook).

....

....

....

....

....

....

....

....

....

....

2.8 Developing an informed personal response to a poem
'Row' by Carol Ann Duffy

Carol Ann Duffy, born in 1955, was Britain's Poet Laureate from 2009 to 2019. This meant that it was her responsibility to compose poems at times of important national occasions.

Her poem 'Row' powerfully captures the intensity of feeling and emotion after a row with a lover. The activities below are designed to help you write a personal response to the poem's content, language and structure. Using evidence from the text to support your ideas will enable you to write an informed and critical response.

Row

But when we rowed,
the room swayed and sank down on its knees,
the air hurt and purpled like a bruise,
the sun banged the gate in the sky and fled.

But when we rowed, 5
the trees wept and threw away their leaves,
the day ripped the hours from our lives,
the sheets and pillows shredded themselves on the bed.

But when we rowed,
our mouths knew no kiss, no kiss, no kiss, 10
our hearts were jagged stones in our fists,
the garden sprouted bones, grown from the dead.

But when we rowed,
your face blanked like a page erased of words,
my hands squeezed themselves, burned like verbs, 15
love turned, and ran, and cowered in our heads.

1. Read the poem carefully. Use different colours to highlight and label examples of the following devices used.

   | onomatopoeia | **simile** | personification | metaphor | **hyperbole** |

> **KEY TERMS**
>
> **simile:** where one thing is compared to another. It is easy to spot a simile, as they include the words 'like', 'as' or 'as if'
>
> **hyperbole:** the use of exaggeration for a deliberate effect

2 There are seven examples of **pathetic fallacy** in the poem.

Complete Table 2.9 by writing either the non-human things which react or the verbs used to describe their reactions.

The non-human things that react	Verbs that describe their reactions
1 The room	
2	'hurt and purpled'
3	
4 The trees	
5	
6	'shredded themselves'
7 The garden	

Table 2.9: Non-human things and verbs describing their reactions in 'Row'

> **KEY TERM**
>
> **pathetic fallacy:** when human feelings are given to something non-human, often the weather, to reflect the feelings of a character or the mood of poetry or prose

3 Look at the examples of imagery in questions 1 and 2. Choose **three** of these and write a sentence for each one, commenting on their effects.

a ....

....

b ....

....

c ....

....

4 Duffy personifies love in the final line. What is the effect of the phrase 'cowered in our heads'?

....

....

5 Look at the structure of each stanza of the poem and the use of repetition. How do these add to the impact of the poem?

....

....

....

....

....

....

6 In Table 2.10, there is a list of some particularly striking phrases. Write a comment on the impressions they create of how the row affected the couple.

The first two are completed to help you. Finally, add one of your own in the last row.

Phrase	Impression
'the room swayed'	She is so upset that she feels dizzy.
'the air hurt'	Everything around her now feels painful.
'the sun banged the gate'	
'the trees wept'	
'our hearts were jagged stones'	
'your face blanked'	

Table 2.10: Striking phrases and the impressions they create in 'Row'

7 Use your responses to the activities to write a critical response to the following practice question:

> **In what ways does Duffy vividly convey the experience of quarrelling? Support your ideas with details from the text.** [25]

Use your answers above to plan your response before you start writing.

You should consider:

- the speaker's thoughts and feelings
- the use of words and images
- the speaker's tone of voice
- the poem's structure.

Unit 3
Responding to prose

3.1 Introducing prose

From *Jane Eyre* by Charlotte Brontë

In Unit 7.2 of the Coursebook, there is a detailed analysis of an extract from *Mary Barton: A Tale of Manchester Life* by Elizabeth Gaskell, published in 1848. The following is the opening to *Jane Eyre* by Charlotte Brontë, published in 1847. The two women were writing in the same era and with the same difficulties experienced by women who wanted to explore other experiences beyond marriage and motherhood.

Jane Eyre

There was no possibility of taking a walk that day. We had been wandering, indeed, in the leafless shrubbery an hour in the morning; but since dinner (Mrs Reed, when there was no company, dined early) the cold winter wind had brought with it clouds so sombre, and a rain so penetrating, that further outdoor exercise was now out of the question.

I was glad of it; I never liked long walks, especially on chilly afternoons: dreadful to me was the coming home in the raw twilight, with nipped fingers and toes, and a heart saddened by the chidings[1] of Bessie, the nurse, and humbled by the consciousness of my physical inferiority to Eliza, John, and Georgiana Reed.

The said Eliza, John, and Georgiana were now clustered round their mamma in the drawing-room[2]: she lay reclined on a sofa by the fireside, and with her darlings about her (for the time neither quarrelling nor crying) looked perfectly happy. Me, she had dispensed from joining the group: saying, 'She regretted to be under the necessity of keeping me at a distance; but that until she heard from Bessie, and could discover by her own observation that I was endeavouring in good earnest to acquire a more sociable and child-like disposition, a more attractive and sprightly manner – something lighter, franker, more natural as it were – she really must exclude me from privileges intended only for contented, happy little children.'

'What does Bessie say I have done?' I asked.

'Jane, I don't like cavillers[3] or questioners; besides, there is something truly forbidding in a child taking up her elders in that manner. Be seated somewhere; and until you can speak pleasantly, remain silent.'

A small breakfast-room adjoined the drawing-room, I slipped in there. It contained a bookcase; I soon possessed myself of a volume[4], taking care that it should be one stored with pictures. I mounted

GLOSSARY

[1] **chiding:** telling-off

[2] **drawing-room:** room to sit in during the day

[3] **cavillers:** people who raise silly objections

[4] **volume:** book

3 Responding to prose

into the window-seat: gathering up my feet, I sat cross-legged, and, having drawn the red moreen[5] curtain nearly close, I was shrined in double retirement.

Folds of scarlet drapery shut in my view to the right hand; to the left were the clear panes of glass, protecting, but not separating me from the drear November day. At intervals, while turning over the leaves in my book, I studied the aspect of that winter afternoon. Afar, it offered a pale blank of mist and cloud; near, a scene of wet lawn and storm-beat shrub, with ceaseless rain sweeping away wildly before a long and lamentable blast.

35

40

GLOSSARY

[5] **moreen:** heavy material

You need three different coloured highlighters for the following activities, which will prompt you to start thinking about the way writers introduce characters, setting and themes.

1   Look at the first two paragraphs of the extract (lines 1–11).

   a   Highlight in colour 1 the words and phrases that describe the weather and its effects on the **narrator** (Jane Eyre).

   b   Highlight in colour 2 the words and phrases that reveal how Jane feels about herself.

2   In lines 12–27 the focus is on Jane's aunt, Mrs Reed.

   Highlight in colour 3 any words and phrases in these lines which give the reader information about her character and attitude towards Jane.

3   From line 28 to the end of the extract, Jane has moved into a room away from the others.

   a   Highlight in colour 1 any words that describe the weather.

   b   Look at the words you have highlighted in colour 1 **throughout the extract**. How would you describe the mood that the setting creates in this opening to the novel? Put a circle around any of the following words that seem suitable.

| gloomy   calm   exciting   bleak   hopeful   unwelcoming |

4   Look at the words and phrases about Mrs Reed that you have highlighted in colour 3.

   Write a sentence each about:

   a   Your first impression of Mrs Reed:

   ....

   ....

KEY TERM

narrator: the person telling the story

b Her treatment of Jane:

....

....

5 Look at the words you have highlighted in colour 2 and also relevant information in the previous questions. Write a paragraph about how Brontë creates sympathy for Jane in this opening section of the novel. Think about the voice of the extract as well as the words and phrases you have identified. Remember to use short quotations in your answer.

....

....

....

....

....

3.2 Responding to how writers present characters

From *All the Light We Cannot See* by Anthony Doerr

In Unit 8.1 of the Coursebook, the extract from this novel described how the blind seven-year-old girl, Marie-Laure, struggled to find her way home through the streets of Paris by using the model of the area made by her father. This extract follows on from the account of her first attempt at the seemingly impossible task.

GLOSSARY

[1] **hydrant:** water pipe in the street

[2] **runnel:** gutter

[3] **spars:** rails

All the Light We Cannot See

Tuesday after Tuesday she fails. She leads her father on six-block detours that leave her angry and frustrated and farther from home than when they started. But in the winter of her eighth year, to Marie-Laure's surprise, she begins to get it right. She runs her fingers over the model in their kitchen, counting miniature benches, trees, lampposts, doorways. Every day some new detail emerges—each storm drain, park bench, and hydrant[1] in the model has its counterpart in the real world.   5

Marie-Laure brings her father closer to home before making a mistake. Four blocks three blocks two. And one snowy Tuesday in March, when he walks her to yet another new spot, very close to the banks of the Seine, spins her around three times, and says, 'Take us home,' she realizes that, for the first time since they began this exercise, dread has not come trundling up from her gut.

Instead she squats on her heels on the sidewalk.   10

The faintly metallic smell of the falling snow surrounds her. *Calm yourself. Listen.*

Cars splash along streets, and snowmelt drums through runnels[2]; she can hear snowflakes tick and patter through the trees. She can smell the cedars in the Jardin des Plantes a quarter mile away. Here the Metro hurtles beneath the sidewalk: that's the Quai Saint-Bernard. Here the sky opens up, and she hears the clacking of branches: that's the narrow stripe of gardens behind the Gallery of Paleontology. This, she realizes, must be the corner of the quay and rue Cuvier.

Six blocks, forty buildings, ten tiny trees in a square. This street intersects this street intersects this street. One centimeter at a time.

Her father stirs the keys in his pockets. Ahead loom the tall, grand houses that flank the gardens, reflecting sound.

She says, 'We go left.'

They start up the length of the rue Cuvier. A trio of airborne ducks threads toward them, flapping their wings in synchrony, making for the Seine, and as the birds rush overhead, she imagines she can feel the light settling over their wings, striking each individual feather.

Left on rue Geoffroy Saint-Hilaire. Right on rue Daubenton. Three storm drains four storm drains five. Approaching on the left will be the open ironwork fence of the Jardin des Plantes, its thin spars[3] like the bars of a great birdcage.

Across from her now: the bakery, the butcher, the delicatessen.

'Safe to cross, Papa?'

'It is.'

Right. Then straight. They walk up their street now, she is sure of it. One step behind her, her father tilts his head up and gives the sky a huge smile. Marie-Laure knows this even though her back is to him, even though he says nothing, even though she is blind—Papa's thick hair is wet from the snow and standing in a dozen of angles off his head, and his scarf is draped asymmetrically over his shoulders, and he's beaming up at the falling snow.

They are halfway up rue des Patriarches. They are outside their building. Marie-Laure finds the trunk of the chestnut tree that grows past her fourth-floor window, its bark beneath her fingers.

Old friend.

In another half second her father's hands are in her armpits, swinging her up, and Marie-Laure smiles, and he laughs a pure, contagious laugh, one she will try to remember all her life, father and daughter turning in circles on the sidewalk in front of their apartment house, laughing together while snow sifts through the branches above.

The Coursebook activities used a checklist of bullets outlined at the start of Unit 8 to consider how Doerr presents the characters of Marie-Laure and her father. You looked at what they say, what they do and how they think and feel. Here are similar activities for this extract, which explores **characterisation**.

> **KEY TERM**
>
> **characterisation:** the ways in which writers present their characters

1. In the first two paragraphs, look at what Marie-Laure **does** and how she **feels**. Choose four quotations that show how she gradually succeeds and her changing feelings.

   Quotation 1: ....

   Quotation 2: ....

   Quotation 3: ....

   Quotation 4: ....

2. In line 11, Marie-Laure says to herself that she must 'Listen'. She realises that her sense of hearing is the most important way of finding her way home.

   List all the instances of onomatopoeia you can find in lines 12–16 and say what effect these create in the extract.

   ....

   ....

   ....

   ....

   ....

   ....

3. Marie-Laure also uses another method of working out where she is.

   Look at lines 17–27. What do you notice about her thoughts in these lines?

   ....

   ....

   ....

   ....

   ....

   ....

3 Responding to prose

4   Look at line 29 to the end of the extract. These focus on both Papa and Marie-Laure, what they say, what they do and their appearance.

How does Doerr show their delight at this moment in the novel?
Find four quotations which support this.

Quotation 1: ....

....

....

....

Quotation 2: ....

....

....

....

Quotation 3: ....

....

....

....

Quotation 4: ....

....

....

....

5   Looking at the extracts in both the Coursebook and Workbook, write a plan to answer the following practice question:

How does Doerr movingly portray the relationship between Marie-Laure and Papa? Support your ideas with details from the text. [25]

Make sure your points are supported by quotations from the text.

....

....

....

....

3 Responding to prose

SET TEXT ACTIVITY 1

Both Jane Eyre and Marie-Laure are characters that have been presented in a sympathetic way. Think about the characters in your set text. Choose one that the writer makes you feel sympathy for. Use a mind map to set out examples of this characterisation, each supported by a quotation.

3.3 Responding to theme
From *The Pieces of Silver* by Karl Sealy

This extract immediately follows the extract from the same story in Unit 9.2 of the Coursebook. There, you read about the humiliation of Clement Dovecot by the acting Headmaster. In the extract below, the scene shifts from school to the home of the Dovecot family. The **theme** of poverty is important in the extract. It is clear why Clement was not able to provide a donation for the retiring headmaster.

> **KEY TERM**
>
> **theme:** the main idea or ideas in a text, such as power, identity and heroism

The Pieces of Silver

It was dusk, and the Dovecots were taking their one substantial meal of the day.

No one could think, looking at their home, that threepenny pieces, or even halfpennies, were to be had there for the asking.

The house was a poor, wretched coop of a room, through the black, water-stained shingles[1] of which you could count a dozen blue glimpses of the sky. The walls of the shack were papered with old newspapers and magazines, discoloured with age and stained and spotted from roof to floor, torn in a score of places, to reveal the rotting, worm-eaten boards beneath. The small room was divided by a threadbare cotton screen depicting seagulls soaring up from a sea of faded blue. In the midst of this drab poverty the free, soaring seagulls, and the once gay pictures of the magazine pages were an unkind comment.

The Dovecots were a family of four: Dave and his wife Maud, Clement and his older sister Evelina.

Clement sat on the sanded floor of the poor sitting-room, his plate of rice between his legs; Evelina lolled over the one battered, depreciated mahogany table, picking at the coarse food with an adolescent discontent; Dave Dovecot, a grizzled, gangling[2] labourer, held his plate in his left hand, while with his right he plied his mouth from a peeling metal spoon; at the propped-open window of the room sat Mrs Dovecot, a long thread of a woman whose bones want[3] had picked like an eagle. Her plate was resting on her lap, and she scraped and pecked and foraged her food like a scratching hen, while she took stock of the passers-by.

When Clement had finished, he took up his empty plate and, getting to his feet, went and stowed it away in the dark box of a kitchen. Returning, he slumped down beside his mother's chair and rested his head against her bony thigh.

After a time he said:

'Ma, could I have the threepence I's been asking for Mr Megahey?'

'Hmn. Wa' threepence boy? Why in de name of de Lord must poor starving people got to find threepences for Jim Megahey what's got his belly sitting so pretty wi' fat?' parried[4] Mrs Dovecot, though she knew well enough.

'I's told you and told you and told you, Ma. He's resigning and we've all got to take threepence to give him,' explained Clement patiently once more.

'Hmn. Threepence is a lot o' money for us poor folk. Hmn. Go ax your father. See what *he* says.' Clement got to his feet reluctantly and moved slowly over to where his father was sitting, for he knew from experience that, in parting with money, his father was a far harder nut to crack than his mother.

Dave Dovecot utilised the approach of his son by extending his empty plate. Clement took the plate to the kitchen. Then he turned once more to tackle his father.

'Can I have a threepence, Papa?' he shouted in his father's ear, for the old man was pretty nigh[5] stone deaf.

'Eh-eh! What's that about a fence, Clement?'

This time Clement put his mouth completely into his father's ear and shouted until his dark face grew darker.

'Eh-eh! Don't shout at me,' was all he got for his pains. 'Don't you deafen me. What's that the young varmint[6] says, Maud?'

Mrs Dovecot came over, and got him to understand after two or three attempts.

'Three pence, Maudie,' he cackled, 'three pence! Did yo' hear that, Maud? Did yo' ever hear the like? I'll bet you ain't never did. Three pence! The lad'll have money what I's got to sweat blood for, just to gi to thet Megahey what's got his bread so well buttered off 'pon both sides not to mention the middle. Three pence! Ha ha! . . . oh Maudie . . .' And he broke down once more in helpless laughter. Clement went out and sat under the breadfruit tree that grew before the door, resting his back against the trunk.

Evelina came to him there when the dusk was thick and sat beside him.

There was a close bond of understanding and companionship between these two. Clement leaned against her so that he could feel the warmth of her arms, warm as the still warm ground beneath him. Biting his nails he told her of his morning's shame.

1 Look again at lines 1–10. List five facts about the Dovecots' home.

Fact 1: ....

Fact 2: ....

Fact 3: ....

Fact 4: ....

Fact 5: ....

GLOSSARY

[1] **shingles:** roof tiles

[2] **gangling:** tall, thin

[3] **want:** poverty

[4] **parried:** replied

[5] **nigh:** almost

[6] **varmint:** badly behaved person

2   'In the midst of this drab poverty the free, soaring seagulls, and the once gay pictures of the magazine pages were an unkind comment.'

   Explain why the narrator says the magazine pictures were 'an unkind comment'.

   ....

   ....

   ....

3   Look at the descriptions Sealy gives of the Dovecot family's poverty. Identify the type of imagery (simile, metaphor, personification) in the phrases in Table 3.1. Then comment on the effects of each use of imagery. In the 'Type of imagery' column, use each of the terms 'simile', 'metaphor' and 'personification' once only.

Phrase	Type of imagery	Effect
'a long thread of a woman whose bones want had picked like an eagle.' (line 16)		
'she scraped and pecked and foraged her food like a scratching hen' (lines 17–18)		
'the dark box of a kitchen' (line 20)		

Table 3.1: Imagery and its effects in *The Pieces of Silver*

3 Responding to prose

4 Write down the impressions of the four characters the writer creates for you in this extract. Use bulleted points.

Clement Dovecot	Dave Dovecot, the father

Maud Dovecot, the mother	Evelina Dovecot, Clement's sister

SET TEXT ACTIVITY 2

Record your initial impressions of characters in your prose set text using the same as in Activity 4.

Character 1	Character 2

Character 3	Character 4

3.4 Exploring setting and mood
From *The Woman in Black* by Susan Hill

Susan Hill (born 1942) is a prize-winning author of many varied books. *The Woman in Black* (published 1983) is one of her most famous books. It is a chilling thriller, telling the story of a young solicitor from London who is sent to settle the affairs of a woman who has recently died. He visits her large, isolated house in the middle of a bleak marsh which gets cut off by the tide every day. In this extract, the solicitor visits the house for the first time.

The Woman in Black

My head reeled at the sheer and startling beauty, the wide, bare openness of it. The sense of space, the vastness of the sky above and on either side made my heart race. I would have travelled a thousand miles to see this. I had never imagined such a place.

The only sounds I could hear above the trotting of the pony's hooves, the rumble of the wheels and the creak of the cart, were sudden, harsh, weird cries from birds near and far. We had travelled perhaps three miles, and passed no farm or cottage, no kind of dwelling house at all, all was emptiness. Then, the hedgerows petered out[1], and we seemed to be driving towards the very edge of the world. Ahead, the water gleamed like metal and I began to make out a track, rather like the line left by the wake[2] of a boat, that ran across it. As we drew nearer, I saw that the water was lying only shallowly over the rippling sand on either side of us, and that the line was in fact a narrow track leading directly ahead, as if into the estuary itself. As we slipped onto it, I realized that this must be the Nine Lives Causeway – this and nothing more – and saw how, when the tide came in, it would quickly be quite submerged and untraceable.

At first the pony and then the trap[3] met the sandy path, the smart noise we had been making ceased, and we went on almost in silence save for a hissing, silky sort of sound. Here and there were clumps of reeds, bleached bone-pale, and now and again the faintest of winds caused them to rattle dryly. The sun at our backs reflected in the water all around so that everything shone and glistened like the surface of a mirror, and the sky had taken on a faint pinkish tinge at the edges, and this in turn became reflected in the marsh and the water. Then, as it was so bright that it hurt my eyes to go on staring at it, I looked up ahead and saw, as if rising out of the water itself, a tall, gaunt house of grey stone with a slate roof, that now gleamed steelily in the light. It stood like some lighthouse or beacon or martello tower[4], facing the whole, wide expanse of marsh and estuary, the most astonishingly situated house I had ever seen or could ever conceivably have imagined, isolated, uncompromising but also, I thought, handsome. As we neared it, I saw the land on which it stood was raised up a little, surrounding it on every side for perhaps three or four hundred yards, of plain, salt-bleached grass, and then gravel. This little island extended in a southerly direction across an area of scrub and field towards what looked like the fragmentary ruins of some old church or chapel.

There was a rough scraping, as the cart came onto the stones, and then pulled up. We had arrived at Eel Marsh House.

For a moment or two, I simply sat looking about me in amazement, hearing nothing save the faint keening[5] of the winter wind that came across the marsh, and the sudden rawk-rawk of a hidden bird. I felt a strange sensation, an excitement mingled with alarm . . . I could not altogether tell what. Certainly, I felt loneliness, for in spite of the speechless Keckwick[6] and the shaggy brown pony I felt quite alone, outside that gaunt, empty house. But I was not afraid – of what could I be afraid in this rare and beautiful spot? The wind? The marsh birds crying? Reeds and still water?

3 Responding to prose

> **GLOSSARY**
>
> [1] **petered out:** slowly disappeared
> [2] **wake:** waves made by a boat
> [3] **trap:** pony-drawn cart
> [4] **martello tower:** watchtower
> [5] **keening:** wailing
> [6] **Keckwick:** the driver of the cart

1. The novel is narrated in the **first person** and this allows the reader to clearly understand and experience the thoughts and feelings of the main character.

    In the first paragraph, find four statements that show how excited and overwhelmed he is to see the setting as he gets near to his house.

    Statement 1: ....

    Statement 2: ....

    Statement 3: ....

    Statement 4: ....

> **KEY TERM**
>
> **first-person narrator:** a narrator telling a story from their point of view, usually using the 'I' pronoun. We see events and other characters through their eyes

2. In lines 4–9, Hill shows how isolated the house is in this setting.

    Complete Table 3.2 with the author's use of devices and the effect they have in the description.

Quotation	Device	Comment on the effect
'the trotting of the pony's hooves, the rumble of the wheels and the creak of the cart'		The clear sound of the pony and cart emphasises how alone they are in the landscape.
'passed no farm or cottage, no kind of dwelling house at all, all was emptiness'	Repetition of 'no' and 'all'	
'we seemed to be driving towards the very edge of the world'		
'the water gleamed like metal'		

Table 3.2: Devices and their effects in *The Woman in Black*

3 Look at lines 11–13 of the extract.

   a   What feeling does the name 'Nine Lives Causeway' convey to you?

   ....

   b   What is the effect in the story of the tide making the Causeway 'quite submerged and untraceable'?

   ....

4 Look at lines 14–19. This moves on to a description of the journey across the marsh which surrounds the house. Comment on the effects created by:

   a   the sounds made by the movement of the pony and trap

   ....

   ....

   b   the metaphor which describes the reeds

   ....

   ....

   c   the description of the sun on the water.

   ....

   ....

5 Look at your answers to questions 2–4. When these are put together, what mood is created by the description of the setting of the marsh?

   ....

   ....

   ....

6 Look at lines 19–27. The narrator finally sees the house. What are the first impressions of the house and its surroundings? Look at the narrator's choice of words and the comparisons he makes.

   ....

   ....

   ....

   ....

   ....

3 Responding to prose

7 'We had arrived at Eel Marsh House.'

    a What is the effect of the short sentence?

    ....

    b What is the effect of the name of the house?

    ....

8 In the last paragraph of the extract, the narrator expresses his reactions to arriving at the house.

    a From this paragraph, find five words that express his initial feelings.

        1 ....

        2 ....

        3 ....

        4 ....

        5 ....

    b How does Hill appeal to the sense of sound in this paragraph, and what effect does it have on the reader?

    ....

    ....

    ....

    c What is the impact of the rhetorical questions that end the extract?

    ....

    ....

    ....

9 Write a paragraph in response to **a** and **b** below, summarising:

    a how Hill creates such a memorable setting

    ....

    ....

    ....

    ....

    ....

b the mood or moods she creates in the whole of the extract.

....

....

....

....

3.5 Exploring a first-person narrative
From *Studies in the Park* by Anita Desai

Anita Desai (born 1937) is an Indian novelist whose novels include *The Village by the Sea* (1982), which is about the changes faced by a small rural community, and *Fasting, Feasting* (1999), which is about the very different lives of sister and brother Uma and Arun.

The following extract is the opening to her short story *Studies in the Park*; it vividly depicts the schoolboy narrator Suno's frustration at the lack of peace and quiet he needs for his studies. In her story, Desai makes use of a first-person narrator. In this case, events are seen from the perspective of the student desperate to study free from the distraction of noise.

Studies in the Park

—Turn it off, turn it off, turn it off! First he listens to the news in Hindi. Directly after, in English. Broom – brroom – brrroom – the voice of doom roars. Next, in Tamil. Then in Punjabi. In Gujarati. What next, my god, what next? Turn it off before I smash it onto his head, fling it out of the window, do nothing of the sort of course, nothing of the sort. 5

—And my mother. She cuts and fries, cuts and fries. All day I hear her chopping and slicing and the pan of oil hissing. What all does she find to fry and feed us on, for God's sake? Eggplants, potatoes, spinach, shoe soles, newspapers, finally she'll slice me and feed me to 10
my brothers and sisters. Ah, now she's turned on the tap. It's roaring and pouring, pouring and roaring into a bucket without a bottom.

—The bell rings. Voices clash, clatter and break. The tin-and-bottle man? The neighbours? The police? The Help-the-Blind man? Thieves and burglars? All of them, all of them, ten or twenty or a hundred of 15
them, marching up the stairs, hammering at the door, breaking in and climbing over me – ten, twenty or a hundred of them.

—Then, worst of all, the milk arrives. In the tallest glass in the house. 'Suno, drink your milk. Good for you, Suno. You need it. Now, before the exams. Must have it, Suno. Drink.' The voice wheedles[1] its 20

GLOSSARY

[1] **wheedles:** tempts by soft words

way into my ear like a worm. I shudder. The table tips over. The milk
runs. The tumbler clangs on the floor. 'Suno, Suno, how will you do
your exams?'

—That is precisely what I ask myself. All very well to give me a
room – Uncle's been pushed off on a pilgrimage to Hardwar[2] to clear
a room for me – and to bring me milk and say 'Study, Suno, study for
your exam.' What about the uproar around me? These people don't
know the meaning of the word Quiet. When my mother fills buckets,
sloshes the kitchen floor, fries and sizzles things in the pan, she thinks
she is being Quiet. The children have never even heard the word, it
amazes and puzzles them. On their way back from school they fling
their satchels in at my door, then tear in to snatch them back before
I tear them to bits. Bawl when I pull their ears, screech when mother
whacks them. Stuff themselves with her fries and then smear the
grease on my books.

So I raced out of my room, with my fingers in my ears, to scream
till the roof fell down about their ears. But the radio suddenly went
off, the door to my parents' room suddenly opened and my father
appeared, bathed and shaven, stuffed and set up with the news of
the world in six different languages – his white *dhoti*[3] blazing, his
white shirt crackling, his patent leather pumps glittering. He stopped
in the doorway and I stopped on the balls of my feet and wavered.
My fingers came out of my ears, my hair came down over my eyes.
Then he looked away from me, took his watch out of his pocket
and enquired, 'Is the food ready?' in a voice that came out of his
nose like the whistle of a punctual train. He skated off towards his
meal, I turned and slouched back to my room. On his way to work,
he looked in to say, 'Remember, Suno. I expect good results from
you. Study hard, Suno.' Just behind him, I saw all the rest of them
standing, peering in, silently. All of them stared at me, at the exam
I was to take. At the degree I was to get. Or not get. Horrifying
thought. Oh study, study, study, they all breathed at me while my
father's footsteps went down the stairs, crushing each underfoot in
turn. I felt their eyes on me, goggling, and their breath on me, hot
with earnestness[4]. I looked back at them, into their open mouths
and staring eyes.

'Study,' I said, and found I croaked. 'I know I ought to study. And
how do you expect me to study – in this madhouse? You run wild,
wild. I'm getting out,' I screamed, leaping up and grabbing my books,
'I'm going to study outside. Even the street is quieter,' I screeched
and threw myself past them and down the stairs that my father had
just cowed[5] and subjugated[6] so that they still lay quivering, and paid
no attention to the howls that broke out behind me of 'Suno, Suno,
listen. Your milk – your studies – your exams, Suno!'

> **GLOSSARY**
>
> [2] **pilgrimage to Hardwar:** journey to an Indian city
>
> [3] ***dhoti*:** traditional Indian dress for men
>
> [4] **earnestness:** seriousness
>
> [5] **cowed:** intimidated
>
> [6] **subjugated:** crushed

CAMBRIDGE IGCSE™ AND O LEVEL LITERATURE IN ENGLISH: WORKBOOK

1 Read the extract carefully. Then look at lines 1–6. Write a short paragraph explaining how Desai creates a vivid opening to the story.

....

....

....

....

....

2 As you read the extract, what impressions do you form of the narrator and his attitude towards his family? Look at the different sections of the story. The story starts with a focus on the father, which then shifts to the mother. Next the bell rings, and so on.

Draw a mind map below to record your impressions about the different sections of the story. Refer briefly to details in the text to support your points.

60

3 Responding to prose

3 Desai uses **stream of consciousness** writing to convey the boy's thoughts and feelings. You see the events and other characters in the story from the boy's perspective. You can see that the writing is in the present tense to give a more immediate impression of Suno's thoughts. Remember that writers make deliberate choices about the language they use.

Highlight examples of the following four sound devices in the extract. Then find one example of each of the devices listed in Table 3.3 and add comments on the specific effects Desai creates by using them.

Device	Example from extract	Comment
Alliteration		
Assonance		
Onomatopoeia		
Rhyme		

Table 3.3: Devices and their effects in *Studies in the Park*

4 The following details from the extract reveal the narrator's thoughts and feelings:
- Lines 4–5: 'Turn it off before I smash it onto his head . . .'
- Line 11: 'Ah, now she's turned on the tap.'
- Lines 27–28: 'These people don't know the meaning of Quiet.'
- Line 54: 'I felt their eyes on me, goggling.'

Highlight (in a different colour) other details in the extract where Desai strikingly captures the narrator's frustration. Then write a plan, using bullet points or a mind map, that would help you to answer this practice question:

> **Explore the ways in which Desai strikingly reveals the narrator's thoughts and feelings about life at home. Support your ideas with details from the text.** [25]

> **KEY TERM**
>
> **stream of consciousness:** a technique used in prose fiction to convey a person's mind as it moves from one thought to another

Plan

3.6 Exploring a third-person narrative
From *Nineteen Eighty-Four* by George Orwell

There is an extract in Unit 11.2 of the Coursebook from *Nineteen Eighty-Four*. Winston, the narrator, gave an unflattering introduction to Tom Parsons during a scene with the Parsons family. Now, a little later in the novel, he appears in person when he is having a meal with Winston and another worker, Syme.

> **GLOSSARY**
> [1] **earmarked:** put aside

Nineteen Eighty-Four

Syme looked up. 'Here comes Parsons,' he said.

Something in the tone of his voice seemed to add, 'that bloody fool.' Parsons, Winston's fellow-tenant at Victory Mansions, was in fact threading his way across the room – a tubby, middle-sized man with fair hair and a froglike face. At thirty-five he was already putting on rolls of fat at neck and waistline, but his movements were brisk and boyish. His whole appearance was that of a little boy grown large, so much so that although he was wearing the regulation overalls, it was almost impossible not to think of him as being dressed in the blue shorts, grey shirt and red neckerchief of the Spies. In visualising him one saw always a picture of dimpled knees and sleeves rolled back from pudgy forearms. Parsons did, indeed, invariably revert to shorts when a community hike or any other physical activity gave him an excuse for doing so. He greeted them both with a cheery 'Hullo, hullo!' and sat down at the table, giving off an intense smell of sweat. Beads of moisture stood out all over his pink face. His powers of sweating were extraordinary. At the Community Centre you could always tell when he had been playing table-tennis by the dampness of the bat handle. Syme had produced a strip of paper on which there was a long column of words, and was studying it with an ink-pencil between his fingers.

'Look at him working away in the lunch hour,' said Parsons, nudging Winston. 'Keenness, eh? What's that you've got there, old boy? Something a bit too brainy for me, I expect. Smith, old boy, I'll tell you why I'm chasing you. It's that sub you forgot to give me.'

'Which sub is that?' said Winston, automatically feeling for money. About a quarter of one's salary had to be earmarked[1] for voluntary subscriptions, which were so numerous that it was difficult to keep track of them.

'For Hate Week. You know – the house-by-house fund. I'm treasurer for our block. We're making an all-out effort – going to put on a tremendous show. I tell you, it won't be my fault if old Victory Mansions doesn't have the biggest outfit of flags in the whole street. Two dollars you promised me.'

Winston found and handed over two creased and filthy notes, which Parsons entered in a small notebook, in the neat handwriting of the illiterate.

'By the way, old boy,' he said. 'I hear that little beggar of mine let fly at you with his catapult yesterday. I gave him a good dressing-down for it. In fact I told him I'd take the catapult away if he does it again.'

1. There were several negative descriptions of Parsons in the extract in the Coursebook. Orwell adds to these in this extract.

   List **five** descriptions which you think have the most impact from lines 2–14.

   a ....

   b ....

   c ....

   d ....

   e ....

2. Find **three** ways in which Orwell portrays Parsons more positively in the lines given below and support your comment with a brief quotation.

   a Lines 15–17: ....

   ....

   b Lines 21–23: ....

   ....

   c Lines 26–28: ....

   ....

3. Although the novel is disturbing and makes many serious points, Orwell also makes it entertaining by his use of **irony**.

   Write notes about how the following show Orwell's use of irony:

   a 'About a quarter of one's salary had to be earmarked for voluntary subscriptions . . .'

   ....

   ....

   b There is to be a celebration with 'flags in the whole street' to mark 'Hate Week'.

   ....

   ....

   c 'the neat handwriting of the illiterate.'

   ....

   ....

> **KEY TERM**
>
> **irony:** a difference between what someone says and what they actually mean, often for comic effect

3 Responding to prose

SAMPLE ANSWER

4 Now look at the student comments about each of the uses of irony. For each pair of comments, say which you think is the better and more insightful by putting a tick against it.

- a i This seems ironic because Winston doesn't want to give so much of his salary to the subscriptions. ☐
- a ii The irony is that everyone is told that they don't have to give the money as it is only 'voluntary', but Winston knows that he actually doesn't have any choice. ☐

- b i Usually flags would be put on a building to celebrate something good, like winning a competition, so it seems ironic that they are celebrating something awful like feeling hate for someone or something and even giving it a whole week to itself. ☐
- b ii It must be a horrible place to live if they are putting flags out to show how everyone likes to hate other people. ☐

- c i Parsons is illiterate, but it is good that he still has neat handwriting. ☐
- c ii Being 'illiterate' means he can hardly read or write, so it is ironic that his writing is neat because it probably doesn't actually make much sense, but it is the best he can manage. ☐

SET TEXT ACTIVITY 3

Find an example of irony in your set text – either in what happens to one of the characters or in the language the writer uses. Note this down along with any quotations needed to support your ideas.

....

....

....

....

....

....

3.7 Developing an informed personal response to a short story

'A Real Durwan' by Jhumpa Lahiri

You studied 'A Real Durwan' in Unit 12 of the Coursebook, which focuses on the structure of a short story and its characters.

This Workbook section will focus on the themes of the story. These refer to the deeper meanings that lie beneath the simpler meanings of the plot. The plot tells of how an elderly woman, an efficient and hard-working doorkeeper, is living in extremely poor conditions and is wrongly accused of helping robbers to steal a basin from the apartment building she looks after.

Before attempting the activities, re-read the story to refresh your memory.

Some themes of the story are:

jealousy	status	truth and lies
community	memories	greed
injustice	responsibility	poverty

1 Complete Table 3.4 by putting one or more of the themes above with the example from the story. You may find that you use some of the themes more than once.

Theme(s)	Example from the story
	The other residents want the same as Mr and Mrs Dalal.
	Boori Ma has to sleep on the roof in the rain.
	The residents wrongly accuse Boori Ma.
	Boori Ma imagines her life in the past.
	Mr Chatterjee wants 'a real durwan'.
	Boori Ma does her job with care and effort.

Table 3.4: Themes in 'A Real Durwan'

3 Responding to prose

2 Themes are linked to the deeper meanings of the story. Using the list of themes in Activity 1, match them to the suggested deeper meanings below. Some may have more than one theme.

   a The residents cannot be satisfied with what they already have.

   ....

   b Boori Ma's lies about her past help her to cope with the present.

   ....

   c Boori Ma has so little in life but makes the best of it with her job.

   ....

   d The residents don't notice Boori Ma's difficulties, even when she is living on the roof.

   ....

   e Mrs Dalal has good intentions but does not carry them through.

   ....

   f The residents are quick to accuse Boori Ma without listening to her.

   ....

3 Sometimes an author uses **symbols** to emphasise themes and convey deeper meanings. In this short story, Lahiri uses Boori Ma's broom and her skeleton keys as symbols to make the reader think more deeply about her character and the meanings of the story.

   a Find **two** quotations from the story that show how and why the broom and skeleton keys are important. Then choose a theme from the list in activity 1 which is linked to each symbol.

   - Boori Ma's broom:
     - Quotation:
       ....
     - Theme:
       ....
   - Her skeleton keys:
     - Quotation:
       ....
     - Theme:
       ....

> **KEY TERM**
>
> **symbol:** a thing that represents, or stands for, something else; in a poem, an idea that has a special or deeper meaning. For example, the use of the heart to represent love

b Write a paragraph showing how Lahiri uses these symbols to help the reader understand Boori Ma's character and feelings. Remember to use your quotations.

....

....

....

....

....

4 Consider the theme of 'status' in the following practice question:

In what ways does Lahiri memorably present status in 'A Real Durwan'? Support your ideas with details from the text. [25]

Table 3.5 contains five statements that you could use in your response.
Below the table are five quotations which support each statement.
Match the correct quotation to each statement.

Statement	Quotation
Boori Ma wants to show that in her past she had a much higher status.	
Mr Dalal wants to improve how he is seen by others.	
Mr Chatterjee thinks that the building and residents should be more respected.	
Boori Ma's status could not get any lower.	
The residents do not want anyone to be thought of as 'better' than them.	

Table 3.5: The theme of status in 'A Real Durwan'

Quotations:

- 'What a building like this needs is a real *durwan*.'
- 'Are the Dalals the only ones who can improve the conditions of this building?'
- 'We had a pond on our property, full of fish.'
- '. . . her lodging below the letter-boxes.'
- ' A sink on the stairwell is sure to impress visitors.'

5 Now choose **one** of the statements from Table 3.5. Write a paragraph developing your chosen statement, to include in an answer to the practice question.
Use further details and quotations from any relevant parts of the story.

....

....

....

....

....

SET TEXT ACTIVITY 4

Choose **two** themes from your set text.

Write a paragraph for each one, showing how it is linked to one of the characters. Include at least **one** quotation in each paragraph.

Theme one:

....

....

....

....

....

....

....

Theme two:

....

....

....

....

....

....

....

> Unit 4

Responding to drama

4.1 Exploring the ways in which dramatists portray characters

From *A Streetcar Named Desire* by Tennessee Williams

Read the extract from *A Streetcar Named Desire* by Tennessee Williams in Unit 15.2 of the Coursebook. Complete the related activities in the Coursebook and then attempt the following activities.

1   What impressions of Blanche do you get from the words she speaks in this extract?

Complete Table 4.1 with four examples and the impressions they give; an example has been given.

Words spoken by Blanche	My impression of her character
'Well – if you'll forgive me – he's *common!*'	Blanche begins by describing Stanley as 'common'. The dash creates a brief pause and Blanche then delivers a short, devastating opinion. By asking for forgiveness, the audience knows beforehand that Blanche is about to say something controversial, but can't stop herself.

Table 4.1: Impressions of Blanche in *A Streetcar Named Desire*

Vivien Leigh playing Blanche in the 1951 film adaptation of *A Streetcar Named Desire*

2   In Table 4.2, list in your own words four things Blanche does not like about Stanley, with evidence from the text.

What Blanche does not like about Stanley	Evidence from the extract

Table 4.2: Things Blanche does not like about Stanley in *A Streetcar Named Desire*

CAMBRIDGE IGCSE™ AND O LEVEL LITERATURE IN ENGLISH: WORKBOOK

3   For the previous two activities, you had to read carefully what the character of Blanche says in the extract.

   For this activity, you will need to read what the **stage directions** tell you about the character of Stanley.

   What picture does the writer create of Stanley from the information provided in the stage directions?

   ....

   ....

   ....

   ....

   ....

   ....

   ....

   ....

> **KEY TERMS**
>
> **stage directions:** written in *italics*, these give details of the set and information about the actors' speech and movements. They are a distinctive feature of drama texts
>
> **third-person narrator:** an omniscient (or all-knowing) narrator. They are able to tell us everything that all characters say, think and do

4   Re-write lines 1–8 of the extract from *A Streetcar Named Desire* as though it were taken from a novel. Write in the **third person**.

   ....

   ....

   ....

   ....

   ....

   ....

   ....

   ....

   ....

   ....

   ....

   ....

4 Responding to drama

5 Re-write lines 31–46 of the extract as though it were taken from a novel.
This time write in the first person as if you are either Blanche or Stanley.

SET TEXT ACTIVITY 1

Choose a short extract that you find particularly powerful from your drama text. The extract should contain stage directions as well as dialogue.

In the space below, re-write the extract as prose fiction.
You may use a first-person or a third-person narrator.

CONTINUED

6   The thinking and writing you did for Activity 5 helped you to **empathise** with the character of Blanche or Stanley.

Name two things that increased your understanding of her character or his and explain why.

> **KEY TERM**
>
> **empathy:** the ability to see things from another's perspective or point of view

4.2 Exploring language and effects
From *Blood Brothers* by Willy Russell

The following extract is from *Blood Brothers* by Willy Russell. The play was first written and presented as a school play in 1981 in Liverpool. Russell then developed the play as a musical, first performed in 1983, and it gradually became a huge hit worldwide.

You will see as you read through the extract that it switches from prose to verse (these parts would be sung in a performance). Using music and song in drama has been common for centuries, and musicals have now become an extremely popular type of drama.

The extract features two contrasting women: Mrs Lyons is a wealthy woman living in a large house in a good area, but she is childless and desperately unhappy about this; Mrs Johnstone is a single mother with many children, recently left by her selfish husband. She lives in poverty in a poor area, earning a small amount of money by cleaning for Mrs Lyons. She has just found out that she is pregnant again, and – worse – is expecting twins.

Willy Russell with the two actresses playing Mrs Lyons and Mrs Johnstone

Blood Brothers

MRS JOHNSTONE, *numbed by the news, moves back to her work, dusting the table upon which the shoes had been placed.*

MRS LYONS *enters.*

MRS LYONS	Hello, Mrs J. How are you?	
	There is no reply.	5
	[*Registering the silence.*] Mrs J? Anything wrong?	
MRS JOHNSTONE	I had it all worked out.	
MRS LYONS	What's the matter?	
MRS JOHNSTONE	We were just getting straight[1].	
MRS LYONS	Why don't you sit down.	10
MRS JOHNSTONE	With one more baby we could have managed. But not with two. The welfare[2] have already been on to me. They say I'm incapable of controllin' the kids I've already got. They say I should put some of them into care[3]. But I won't. I love the bones of every one of them. I'll even love these two when they come along. But like they say at the welfare, kids can't live on love alone.	15
MRS LYONS	Twins? You're expecting twins?	20
	The NARRATOR *enters.*	

GLOSSARY

[1] **getting straight:** becoming more secure financially

[2] **the welfare:** the authorities who make sure children are being looked after properly

[3] **into care:** placed in large homes run by the authorities for children

NARRATOR	How quickly an idea, planted, can Take root and grow into a plan. The thought conceived in this very room Grew as surely as a seed, in a mother's womb. *The NARRATOR exits.*	25
MRS LYONS	[*almost inaudibly*] Give one of them to me.	
MRS JOHNSTONE	What?	
MRS LYONS	[*containing her excitement*] Give one of them to me.	30
MRS JOHNSTONE	Give one to you?	
MRS LYONS	Yes . . . yes.	
MRS JOHNSTONE	[*taking it almost as a joke*] But y' can't just . . .	
MRS LYONS	When are you due[4]?	
MRS JOHNSTONE	Erm, well, about . . . Oh, but Mrs . . .	35
MRS LYONS	Quickly, quickly, tell me . . . when are you due?	
MRS JOHNSTONE	July he said, the beginning of . . .	
MRS LYONS	July . . . and my husband doesn't get back until the middle of July. He need never guess . . .	
MRS JOHNSTONE	[*amused*] Oh, it's mad . . .	40
MRS LYONS	I know, it is. It's mad . . . but it's wonderful, it's perfect. Look, look, you're what, four months pregnant, but you're only just beginning to show . . . so, so I'm four months pregnant and I'm only just beginning to show. [*She grabs a cushion and arranges it beneath her dress.*] Look, look. I could have got pregnant just before he went away. But I didn't tell him in case I miscarried, I didn't want to worry him whilst he was away. But when he arrives home I tell him we were wrong, the doctors were wrong. I have a baby, our baby. Mrs Johnstone, it will work, it will if only you'll . . .	45 50
MRS JOHNSTONE	Oh, Mrs Lyons, you can't be serious.	
MRS LYONS	You said yourself, you said you had too many children already.	55
MRS JOHNSTONE	Yeh, but I don't know if I wanna give one away.	

GLOSSARY

[4] **due:** the date the baby will be born

MRS LYONS	Already you're being threatened by the welfare people. Mrs Johnson, with two more children how can you possibly avoid some of them being put into care? Surely, it's better to give one child to me. Look, at least if the child was with me you'd be able to see him every day, as you came to work.	60

She stares at MRS JOHNSTONE, *willing her to agree.*   65

MRS LYONS	Please, Mrs Johnstone. Please.
MRS JOHNSTONE	Are y'... are y' that desperate to have a baby?
MRS LYONS	[*singing*]
	Each day I look out from this window
	I see him with his friends, I hear him call, 70
	I rush down but as I fold my arms around him,
	He's gone. Was he ever there at all?
	I've dreamed of all the places I would take him,
	The games we'd play, the stories I would tell,
	The jokes we'd share, the clothing I would make him, 75
	I reach out. But as I do. He fades away.

The melody shifts into that of MRS JOHNSTONE *who is looking at* MRS LYONS, *feeling for her.* MRS LYONS *gives her a half-smile and a shrug, perhaps slightly embarrassed at what she has revealed.* MRS JOHNSTONE *turns and looks at the room she is in. Looking up in awe at the comparative opulence[5] and ease of the place. Tentatively and wondering she sings*:   80

MRS JOHNSTONE	If my child was raised
	In a palace like this one, 85
	[He] wouldn't have to worry where
	His next meal was comin' from.
	His clothing would be [supplied by]
	George Henry Lee[6].

MRS LYONS *sees that* MRS JOHNSTONE *might be persuaded.*   90

MRS LYONS	[*singing*] He'd have all his own toys
	And a garden to play in.
MRS JOHNSTONE	He could make too much noise
	Without the neighbours complainin'.
MRS LYONS	Silver trays to take meals on. 95

GLOSSARY

[5] **opulence:** luxury

[6] **George Henry Lee:** a good department store

MRS JOHNSTONE	A bike with *both* wheels on?	
MRS LYONS *nods enthusiastically.*		
MRS LYONS	And he'd sleep every night In a bed of his own.	
MRS JOHNSTONE	He wouldn't get into fights He'd leave matches alone. And you'd never find him Effin' and blindin'[7]. And when he grew up He could never be told To stand and queue up For hours on end at the dole[8] He'd grow up to be	100 105
MRS LYONS and **MRS JOHNSTONE** [*together*]		
	A credit to me.	110
MRS JOHNSTONE	To you. I would still be able to see him every day, wouldn't I?	
MRS LYONS	Of course.	
MRS JOHNSTONE	An'... an' you would look after him, wouldn't y'?	115
MRS LYONS	[*singing*] I'd keep him warm in winter And cool when it shines. I'd pull out his splinters Without making him cry. I'd always be there If his dream was a nightmare. My child. My child.	 120

> **GLOSSARY**
>
> [7] **Effin' and blindin':** swearing
>
> [8] **the dole:** where money is given to those who can't find jobs

4 Responding to drama

1   Read the extract through aloud (in pairs, if possible). You may need to do this twice to understand how this is a major turning point in the play.

    a   Summarise exactly what is happening in the extract.

    ....

    ....

    ....

    ....

    b   What is the role and effect of the narrator?

    ....

    ....

    ....

    ....

2   Look back at the speeches that are in verse. Imagine the actresses singing these.

    a   What effects would this create for the audience?

    ....

    ....

    b   More generally, what are the advantages of having music or song in a play alongside the spoken words?

    ....

    ....

    ....

3   This extract emphasises the advantages the baby would have if brought up by Mrs Lyons. It lists more than ten of these in the verse section between lines 68 and 108. Choose five advantages which you think make the most compelling argument and write the quotations for them.

    1   ....

    2   ....

    3   ....

    4   ....

    5   ....

4   Find an example of each of the following devices in Table 4.3 and say what effect it has at that point in the extract.

Device	Quotation	Comment on effect
Repetition		
Simile		
Metaphor		
The use of questions		
The use of short sentences		

Table 4.3: Devices and their effects in *Blood Brothers*

5   The focus of the extract is the decision facing the two women. Write a paragraph for each of them, analysing how Russell shows aspects of their characters and how he makes you feel about them. Remember to support your points with short quotations.

Mrs Johnstone:

....

....

....

....

....

....

....

4 Responding to drama

Mrs Lyons:

....

....

....

....

....

....

....

6 Russell is also making some deeper points about the way the two women live. Write down one possible deeper meaning from this part of the play.

....

....

....

4.3 Recapping a character from a drama text

> **SET TEXT ACTIVITY 2**
>
> The activities below can be used as a recapping exercise for characters from your drama texts.
>
> For these activities choose **one** character. Make sure you include page references so you can easily find the relevant page and any useful quotations again.
>
> a What do the stage directions and dialogue reveal about the character's appearance?
>
> ....
> ....
> ....
> ....
> ....
> ....
>
> b What do the stage directions tell you about the character's personal qualities?
>
> ....
> ....
> ....
> ....
> ....
> ....
>
> c What are your first impressions of the character from their first appearance on stage and from their first lines?
>
> ....
> ....
> ....
> ....

CONTINUED

d Does your view of the character change during the course of the play? If so, when, why and how?

e How does the character contrast with other characters?

f Comment on any conflict the character has with one or more other characters.

4.4 Writing a critical essay on your chosen character

SET TEXT ACTIVITY 3

Use your answers to Set text activity 2, parts **a–f**, in the previous section to help you answer the following practice question:

> **In what ways does the writer make this character so memorable in the play? Support your ideas with details from the text.** [25]

Insert the names of your writer and character below:

In what ways does .... make .... so memorable in the play?

a   List ten quotations you could use in your answer and highlight the key words.

- ....
- ....
- ....
- ....
- ....
- ....
- ....
- ....

CONTINUED

-
-

b Write your answer to the practice question.

CONTINUED

4.5 Exploring language and structure
From 'Master Harold'... and the Boys by Athol Fugard

The following extract is from 'Master Harold'... and the Boys by Athol Fugard, first produced in 1982. It is set in South Africa in 1950 during the era of Apartheid, when there was extreme racism towards Black people, who had to live there under very restrictive rules. Fugard is known for his political plays, and was part of the Anti-Apartheid Movement, refusing for his plays to be shown in theatres which excluded 'non-whites'.

The play is set in a teashop owned by Hally's parents, where two Black servants, Sam and Willie, work. Hally (aged 17) is white; he has arrived there after school and is chatting to the men. In this part of the play, he is thinking back to a time when he was younger and Sam made him a kite. The play, including this extract, contains language that shows the subtle forms of everyday racism that were 'normalised' in South Africa during Apartheid.

Three actors in a 1983 staging of the play

'Master Harold'... and the Boys

HALLY   See what's cooking in Sam's room. This time it was you on the floor. You had two thin pieces of wood and you were smoothing them down with a knife. It didn't look particularly interesting, but when I asked you what you were doing, you just said, 'Wait and see, Hally. Wait... and see.'... in that secret sort of way of yours, so I knew there was a surprise coming. You teased me, by being deliberately slow and not answering my questions!

[*SAM laughs.*]

HALLY   And whistling while you worked away! God, it was infuriating! I could have brained you![1] It was only when you tied them together in a cross and put that down on the brown paper that I realized what you were doing. Sam is making a kite! And when I asked you, you said: Yes...! [*shaking his head with disbelief*] The sheer audacity of it took my breath away. I mean seriously, what does a black man know[2] about flying a kite? I'll be honest with you, Sam, I had no hopes for it. If you think I was excited and happy, you got another guess coming. In fact I was scared that we were going to make fools of ourselves. When we left the boarding house to go up onto the hill, I was praying quietly that there wouldn't be any other kids around to laugh at us.

SAM   [*enjoying the memory as much as HALLY*] Ja[3], I could see that.

HALLY   I made it obvious, did I?

GLOSSARY

[1] **brained you:** hit you on the head

[2] **what does a black man know:** this is an example of the everyday racism that was prevalent and 'normalised' during Apartheid

[3] **Ja:** Yes

SAM	Ja. He refused to carry it.	
HALLY	Do you blame me? Can you remember what the poor thing looked like? Tomato-box wood and brown paper! Flour and water for glue! Two of my mother's old stockings for a tail and then all those bits and pieces of string you made me tie together so that we could fly it! That was now only asking for a miracle to happen.	30
SAM	Then the big argument when I told you to hold the string and run with it when I let go.	35
HALLY	I was prepared to run alright, but straight back to the boarding house.	
SAM	[*knowing what's coming*] So what happened?	
HALLY	Come on Sam, you remember as well as I do.	
SAM	I want to hear it from you.	40
HALLY	[*Pauses; wants to be as accurate as possible.*] You went a little distance from me down the hill, you held it up ready to let it go . . . This is it I thought. Like everything else in my life, here comes another fiasco[4]. Then you shouted, 'Go Hally!' and I started to run. [*another pause*] I don't know how to describe it, Sam. Ja! The miracle happened! I was running, waiting for it to crash to the ground, but instead suddenly there was something alive behind me at the end of the string, tugging at it as if it wanted to be free. I looked back . . . [*Shakes his head*.] . . . I still can't believe my eyes. It was flying! Looping around and trying to climb even higher into the sky. You shouted to me to let it have more string. I did, until there was none left, and I was just holding that piece of wood we had tied it to. You came up and joined me. You were laughing.	45 50 55
SAM	So were you. And shouting, 'It works, Sam! We've done it.'	
HALLY	And we had! I was so proud of us! It was the most splendid thing I had ever seen. I wished there were hundreds of kids around to watch us. The part that scared me though, was when you showed me how to make it dive down to the ground and then swoop up again, just when it was on the point of crashing.	60
SAM	He didn't want to try, himself.	
HALLY	Of course not! Watching you do it made me nervous enough. I was quite happy just to see it up there with its tail fluttering behind it. You left me after that, didn't you? You explained how to get it down, we tied it to the bench so that I could sit and watch it, and you went away. I wanted you to stay, you know. I was a little scared of having to look after it by myself.	65

> **GLOSSARY**
> [4] **fiasco:** disaster

SAM	[*quietly*] I had work to do, Hally.	70
HALLY	It was sort of sad bringing it down, Sam. And it looked sad again when it was lying there on the ground. Like something that had lost its soul. Just tomato-box wood, brown paper and two of my mother's old stockings! But I'll never forget that first moment when I saw it up there. I had a stiff neck the next day from looking up so much.	75

1. The extract is structured as a conversation in the present between Hally and Sam in which Fugard uses a **flashback** to a time when Hally was a young boy. He is remembering when Sam made him a kite. Read the extract aloud; most of it is spoken by Hally and is almost a **monologue**.

   Within this flashback, there are four clear divisions to the story. For each one, find two key quotations that express Hally's mood during each part.

> **KEY TERMS**
>
> **flashback:** a scene or memory that takes the narrative back to something that happened in the past
>
> **monologue:** a long speech delivered by one character

Making the kite

1 ....

2 ....

His mood: ....

Taking the kite up onto the hill

1 ....

2 ....

His mood: ....

Flying the kite

1 ....

2 ....

His mood: ....

Bringing the kite down and immediately afterwards

1 ....

2 ....

His mood: ....

2 Although Sam says very little in the extract, find three quotations which show his enjoyment in listening to Hally and remembering the past.

   1 ....

   2 ....

   3 ....

3 The kite itself almost becomes a character in the story.

   Write a paragraph showing how Fugard's description of the kite, through Hally's account, emphasises its importance to both the characters and to the deeper meanings.

   Consider the descriptions of how it is made and the imagery used once it is in the air and then on the ground again. Think about what the kite might symbolise to Hally and Sam.

   ....

   ....

   ....

   ....

   ....

   ....

   ....

   ....

   ....

   ....

   ....

   ....

   ....

   ....

   ....

4.6 Exploring themes in a drama text

SET TEXT ACTIVITY 4

Choose a main theme from one of your drama texts, and then complete the following activities.

a   Complete Figure 4.1 with the relevant information for your chosen theme.

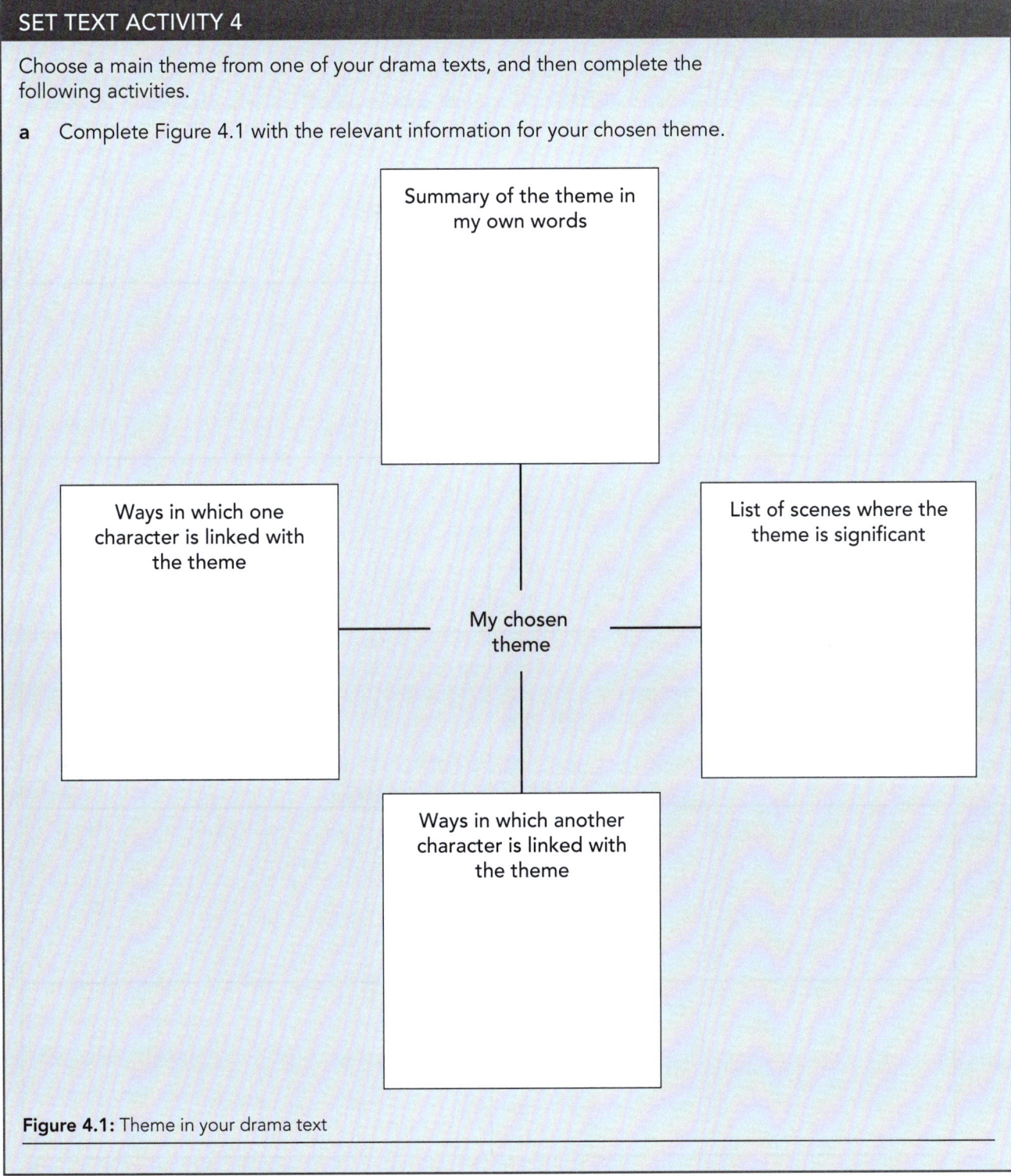

Figure 4.1: Theme in your drama text

> **CONTINUED**

b In Table 4.4, add a list of key quotations for your theme and make comments about the effects of the key words in the quotations.

Quotation	Comment

Table 4.4: Theme in your drama text

> Unit 5

Writing skills

5.1 Critical writing

The activities in this section of the Workbook should be attempted after reading Unit 17 in the Coursebook.

The activities here will help you with the following:

1 Recognising the difference between assertion and analysis, as you provide evidence from the text to support your ideas.

2 Exploring ways in which writers achieve specific effects in their writing such as:

- how they create a certain mood
- how they use imagery and sound to convey their ideas
- how they use structure to build suspense
- how they use narrative perspective to capture a character's thoughts and feelings.

From *Strange Case of Dr Jekyll and Mr Hyde* by Robert Louis Stevenson

The following extract is from the prose novel *Strange Case of Dr Jekyll and Mr Hyde*, written by Scottish writer Robert Louis Stevenson in 1886.

In this extract, the third-person narrator tells the disturbing story of the murder by Mr Hyde of a gentleman of high social rank. The narrator relies heavily in his account of the incident on the experience of the maid who witnessed it; you can tell this from the information in the three sets of brackets in the extract.

The activities that follow the extract offer further opportunities to practise skills for exploring prose texts, whether for unseen or set prose texts. As you read the extract, consider the following practice question:

> **In what ways does Stevenson make this such a shocking incident? Support your ideas with details from the text.** [25]

Strange Case of Dr Jekyll and Mr Hyde

Nearly a year later, in the month of October, 18—, London was startled by a crime of singular ferocity[1] and rendered all the more notable by the high position[2] of the victim. The details were few and startling. A maidservant living alone in a house not far from the river, had gone upstairs to bed about eleven. Although a fog rolled over the city in the small hours, the early part of the night was cloudless, and the lane, which the maid's window overlooked, was brilliantly lit by the full moon. It seems she was romantically given, for she sat down upon her box, which stood immediately under the window, and fell

5

GLOSSARY

[1] **ferocity:** extreme fierceness

[2] **high position:** high social rank

into a dream of musing. Never (she used to say, with streaming tears, when she narrated that experience), never had she felt more at peace with all men or thought more kindly of the world. And as she so sat she became aware of an aged and beautiful gentleman with white hair, drawing near along the lane; and advancing to meet him, another and very small gentleman, to whom at first she paid less attention. When they had come within speech (which was just under the maid's eyes) the older man bowed and accosted the other with a very pretty manner of politeness. It did not seem as if the subject of his address were of great importance; indeed, from his pointing, it sometimes appeared as if he were only inquiring his way; but the moon shone on his face as he spoke, and the girl was pleased to watch it, it seemed to breathe such an innocent and old-world kindness of disposition, yet with something high too, as of a well-founded self-content. Presently³ her eye wandered to the other, and she was surprised to recognise in him a certain Mr Hyde, who had once visited her master and for whom she had conceived a dislike. He had in his hand a heavy cane, with which he was trifling⁴; but he answered never a word, and seemed to listen with an ill-contained impatience. And then all of a sudden he broke out in a great flame of anger, stamping with his foot, brandishing the cane, and carrying on (as the maid described it) like a madman. The old gentleman took a step back, with the air of one very much surprised and a trifle hurt; and at that Mr Hyde broke out of all bounds and clubbed him to the earth. And next moment, with ape-like fury, he was trampling his victim under foot and hailing down a storm of blows, under which the bones were audibly shattered and the body jumped upon the roadway. At the horror of these sights and sounds, the maid fainted.

GLOSSARY

³ **presently:** before long

⁴ **trifling:** behaving in a way that isn't serious

1 Read from 'A maidservant living alone' (line 4) to 'or thought more kindly of the world' (line 12).

   What mood does the writer create in these lines? Make brief notes that answer the question. Use short quotations to support your points.

   • ....

   • ....

   • ....

   • ....

   • ....

5 Writing skills

2. Read from 'And as she so sat' (line 12) to 'a well-founded self-content' (line 23).

   What impressions do you form of the old man? Complete Table 5.1 with quotations that support your impressions.

Quotation	Impression
'an aged and beautiful gentleman'	

   Table 5.1: Impressions of the old man in *Strange Case of Dr Jekyll and Mr Hyde*

3. Read from 'He had in his hand a heavy cane' (line 26) to the end of the extract.

   Explore the language devices the writer uses to portray the violence of Mr Hyde's attack. You might focus on imagery and sound devices. Complete Table 5.2 with your impressions of the language devices used.

Device	Comment
Metaphor in 'great flame of anger'	

   Table 5.2: Language devices in *Strange Case of Dr Jekyll and Mr Hyde*

4 Using your answers to activities 1–3, write a plan for your answer to the practice question, **in what ways does Stevenson make this such a shocking incident?** Consider also the writer's use of:

- the maid's perspective in the account of the attack
- structure in the extract to create suspense
- contrasts in mood and presentation of the two characters.

5.2 Approaching assessment

You will now be familiar from both the Coursebook and this Workbook with the skills needed as you approach questions in assessment, whether on poems, prose and drama texts or unseen poem and prose extracts. The poem and activities that follow provide further, final practice of these skills. You will follow the route you have been practising with essay questions:

- annotating the question and the poem
- making a detailed plan
- then using the 'Point, quotation and comment' model to write your answer.

'High Flight (an Airman's Ecstasy)' by John Gillespie Magee Jr.

John Gillespie Magee Jr. (1922–1941) was a fighter pilot with the Royal Canadian Air Force, flying Spitfire planes. He tragically died in a flying accident. The poem celebrates the high-altitude flights which Magee found so inspirational.

High Flight (an Airman's Ecstasy)

Oh, I have slipped the surly[1] bonds[2] of earth
And danced the skies on laughter-silvered wings;
Sunward I've climbed and joined the tumbling mirth
Of sun-split clouds – and done a hundred things
You have not dreamed of; wheeled and soared and swung   5
High in the sun-lit silence. Hovering there
I've chased the shouting wind along, and flung
My eager craft[3] through footless halls of air;
Up, up the long, delirious[4], burning blue
I've topped the wind-swept heights with easy grace,   10
Where never lark nor even eagle flew;
And while, with silent lifting mind I've trod
The high untrespassed[5] sanctity[6] of space,
Put out my hand, and touched the face of God.

GLOSSARY

[1] **surly:** bad-tempered

[2] **bonds:** things which tie or restrain

[3] **craft:** aircraft, plane

[4] **delirious:** wildly excited

[5] **untrespassed:** not intruded upon

[6] **sanctity:** sacredness, holiness

CAMBRIDGE IGCSE™ AND O LEVEL LITERATURE IN ENGLISH: WORKBOOK

1 Read the poem and its title carefully, and then consider how you might answer the following practice question:

   **Explore how Magee vividly depicts the speaker's joy of flying.
   Support your ideas with details from the text.** [25]

   Read the question carefully. Which are the key words in the question?

   ....

   ....

2 The question asks for comment on the joy of flying. Annotate the poem by highlighting particularly vivid words and phrases which show this.

3 a List the words that describe the movement of the plane.

   ....

   ....

   b What is the effect of these words? Make sure that your comment is answering the question.

   ....

   ....

4 Complete Table 5.3 using words and phrases you have annotated. You may use more than one example for each device.

The poet's use of:	Example(s)	The effect(s) created
Alliteration		
Personification		
Caesura		
Enjambment		

Table 5.3: Devices and their effects in 'High Flight (an Airman's Ecstasy)'

5 a   What is the impact of the first line?

....

....

  b   What is the impact of the final line?

....

....

6   Why does the speaker mention the birds in line 11?

....

....

....

7   Find quotations that convey the idea of being alone and at peace in the sky.

....

....

....

....

8   List below any other **relevant** points and quotations you have not already used and the effects they create, for example, about structure.

....

....

....

....

....

....

....

....

9 Number the points made in activities 3 to 8 in the most logical and effective order for your essay. Check that all of them are relevant to the question.

Now, use the 'Point, quotation and comment' model to write your essay, following the order of the plan you have made. Remember that you can alter and adjust this as you write – a plan is a guide for you to remain focused on the question and not forget important points, but you do not have to stick rigidly to it. Check your writing when you have finished.

Glossary

alliteration: the repetition of consonant sounds in words that are close together. For example, 'Sudden successive flights of bullets streak the silence'

annotate: to make notes, providing brief explanations or comments

assonance: the repetition of vowel sounds in words which are placed close together

caesura: a deliberate pause or stop in a line of poetry

characterisation: the ways in which writers present their characters

empathy: the ability to see things from another person's perspective or point of view

enjambment: where lines run on without punctuation and without a break in the meaning

first-person narrator: a narrator telling a story from their point of view, usually using the 'I' pronoun. We see events and other characters through their eyes

flashback: a scene or memory that takes the narrative back to something that happened in the past

form: the overall structure of a poem. This can include the length of lines, the rhythm and the system of repetition and rhyme

free verse: poetry with no regular rhyming pattern, line length or rhythm. This is the most common form in more modern poetry

genre: a specific type of drama or literature, for example, science fiction, romance, spy, war, fantasy or horror

hyperbole: the use of exaggeration for a deliberate effect

imagery: a literary device where writers use vivid description to appeal to the reader's senses and create images in their mind. It plays a central role in poetry

irony: a difference between what someone says and what they actually mean, often for comic effect

metaphor: a literary device that says that one thing is actually another, rather than using words such as 'like' to compare things. For example, in Wilfred Owen's poem 'Exposure', the burning coal in fires is described as 'dark-red jewels'

monologue: a long speech delivered by one character

narrator: the person telling the story

octave: the first eight lines of a sonnet

onomatopoeia: a word that sounds like the thing it describes. For example, 'buzz' in 'The bee buzzed in my ear'

pathetic fallacy: when human feelings are given to something non-human, often the weather, to reflect the feelings of a character or the mood of poetry or prose

personification: when something inanimate is given human characteristics. For example, 'Our brains ache, in the merciless iced east winds that knive us'

rhetorical question: a type of question that does not require an answer, since this is usually obvious from the question. The purpose of a rhetorical question is to emphasise a point

sestet: the final six lines of a sonnet

simile: where one thing is compared to another. It is easy to spot a simile, as they include the words 'like', 'as' or 'as if'

sonnet: a poem of 14 lines, each having 10 syllables

stage directions: written in **italics**, these give details of the set and information about the actors' speech and movements. They are a distinctive feature of drama texts

stanza: a group of lines within a poem

stream of consciousness: a technique used in prose fiction to convey a person's mind as it moves from one thought to another

symbol: a thing that represents, or stands for, something else; in a poem, an idea that has a special or deeper meaning. For example, the use of the heart to represent love

theme: the main idea or ideas in a text, such as power, identity and heroism

third-person narrator: an omniscient (or all-knowing) narrator. They are able to tell us everything that all characters say, think and do

> Acknowledgements

The authors and publishers acknowledge the following sources of copyright material and are grateful for the permissions granted. While every effort has been made, it has not always been possible to identify the sources of all the material used, or to trace all copyright holders. If any omissions are brought to our notice, we will be happy to include the appropriate acknowledgements on reprinting.

Unit 2 'Home after three months away' by Robert Lowell from *Selected Poems* published by Farrar, Straus and Giroux, Inc. © 2003 by Harriet and Sheridan Lowell; 'Sonnet' by Elizabeth Bishop published in *Collected Poems* by Farrar, Straus and Giroux, Inc.; '300 Goats' by permission of the author, Naomi Shihab Nye, 2025; 'Out, Out –' by Robert Frost from THE POETRY OF ROBERT FROST edited by Edward Connery Lathem. Copyright © 1916, 1969 by Henry Holt and Company. Copyright © 1944 by Robert Frost. Reprinted by permission of Henry Holt and Company. All Rights Reserved. 'Row' from *Rapture* by Carol Ann Duffy, 2006, published by Pan Macmillan Ltd.; **Unit 3** Excerpt from *All The Light We Cannot See* by Anthony Doerr. Copyright © 2014 by Anthony Doerr. Reprinted with the permission of Scribner, an imprint of Simon & Schuster LLC. All rights reserved and HarperCollins Publishers Ltd.; Excerpt from 'The Pieces of Silver' by Karl Sealy – "As sons of Karl and Beryl Sealy, we, Roger and Trevor Sealy, wish to express our heartfelt thanks to our parents, who, with God's help, raised us to honour and continue the life's work of our father, Karl Sealy. Today, new generations can once again journey into the world of his timeless short stories and discover the brilliance of his writing. A special thank you goes out to Cambridge for helping us to keep these stories alive."; Excerpt from *The Woman in Black* by Susan Hill published by Vintage. Copyright © 1983. Reprinted by permission of Penguin Books Limited/The Random House Group Limited and reprinted permission of Peters Fraser & Dunlop on behalf of Susan Hill; Excerpt from 'Studies in the Park' from *Games at Twilight* by Anita Desai; Abridged excerpt from *1984* by George Orwell. Copyright © 1949 by Harcourt, Inc. and renewed 1977 by Sonia Brownell Orwell. Used by permission of HarperCollins Publishers; **Unit 4** Excerpt from *Blood Brothers* © Willy Russell, 1985, Methuen Drama, an imprint of Bloomsbury Publishing Plc.; Abridged excerpt from *Master Harold and the Boys* by Athol Fugard, 1982; 'High Flight' by Magee, John Gillespie. "Letter to Parents," September 3, 1941. John Magee Papers, Library of Congress, Washington, D.C.

Thanks to the following for permission to reproduce images:

Cover Pchyburrs/Getty Images

Inside **Unit 1** Maskot/GI; Claes Touber/GI; **Unit 2** Photos.com/GI; Charliebishop/GI; V_zaitsev/GI; Raw-Pix/GI; Jeremy Poland/GI; Liam Norris/GI; **Unit 3** Michael Ochs Archives/Handout/GI; Marcia Straub/GI; Umesh negi/GI; **Unit 4** Hulton Archive/GI; Mirrorpix/GI; Sergiy1975/GI; Ilbusca/GI; Donald Cooper/Photostage; **Unit 5** Rancho_runner/GI

Key: GI = Getty Images